FAMILY AND CONSUMER SCIENCE 6
INTERIOR DECORATING

CONTENTS

Author: Marcia Parker, M.Ed.
Editor: Alan Christopherson, M.S.
Illustrations: Alpha Omega Graphics

Alpha Omega Publications®

804 N. 2nd Ave. E., Rock Rapids, IA 51246-1759
© MM by Alpha Omega Publications, Inc.   All rights reserved.
LIFEPAC is a registered trademark of Alpha Omega Publications, Inc.

INTERIOR DECORATING

People have been decorating their homes for thousands of years. In museums all over the world, you can see examples of furniture and decorations from ancient civilizations that were discovered by archaeologists. Below is an example of an Egyptian throne and a first-century Roman table found in the excavations of Pompeii.

Egyptian throne   **Roman table**

There are many restorations of entire settlements throughout the United States that depict the furniture and decorations used during specific time periods. Some of the more famous places to visit are Sturbridge Village, Plymouth, and Williamsburg. Other great examples of historical decorations can be seen by visiting some of the homes of the early presidents, such as George Washington's Mt. Vernon or Thomas Jefferson's Monticello. These restorations are wonderful tributes to our past. Take the opportunity to visit them should you ever have the chance.

There are also many castles and museums around the world that exemplify historical decoration, such as the many European castles.

In this LIFEPAC®, you will learn about some of the more important historical periods of decoration and about the changes that have brought us to modern interior decoration.

You will also be given the opportunity to develop and polish your skills at designing and decorating your own bedroom, at least on paper. In order to do this, we will review the elements and principles of design as they relate to interior decorating. You will learn specific techniques for interior design and special treatments to enhance your endeavors. You will learn to use two- and three-dimensional effects to enrich your efforts.

The last section of this LIFEPAC will give you a chance to show your skill at sewing a pillow that will complement the bedroom you have designed. This LIFEPAC should challenge you by sending you down the path of a new and exciting adventure.

Note: All vocabulary words in this LIFEPAC appear in **boldface** print the first time they are used. If you are unsure of the meaning when you are reading, study the definitions given in the glossary.

OBJECTIVES

Read these objectives. The objectives tell you what you will be able to do when you have successfully finished this LIFEPAC.

When you have finished this LIFEPAC, you should be able to:

1. Gain knowledge in the history of furniture and interior design.

2. Identify pieces of furniture and interior decor from the various periods and countries.

3. Gain an understanding of how the interior decorations of other countries influenced American interior decorations.

4. Explain the elements and principles of design as they pertain to interior decoration.

5. Gain skills in practical techniques of interior decoration.

6. Learn the basics of furniture arrangement from room to room.

7. Gain knowledge concerning the woods used in making furniture.

8. Gain understanding in specific treatments such as floors and floor coverings, walls, windows, and lighting.

9. Demonstrate skill in producing visual enrichment through two-dimensional and three-dimensional objects.

10. Document in a notebook how you would design your bedroom.

11. Learn the basics about sewing for the home.

12. Design and sew a pillow that will complement the decor of your newly designed bedroom.

Survey the LIFEPAC. Ask yourself some questions about the study. Write your questions here.

_____

_____

_____

_____

_____

_____

_____

_____

_____

I. A BRIEF HISTORY OF INTERIOR DECORATION

As we look at the history of interior decoration, we will divide the information into the following sections: continental decoration, English decoration, traditional American decoration, and twentieth-century decoration. It will be easy to see the strong influence the continental countries of France, Germany, and Spain had on American decor. However, no country has influenced American interior decoration as much as England. English period styles of furniture and decorations are used in many American homes, with either original antiques or reproductions.

Section Objectives

Review these objectives. When you have completed this section, you should be able to:

1. Gain knowledge in the history of furniture and interior design.

2. Identify pieces of furniture and interior decor from the various periods and countries.

3. Gain an understanding of how the interior decorations of other countries influenced American interior decorations.

CONTINENTAL DESIGN

France. France, a leader in clothing design, is also considered a leader in Europe of interior furniture design. The French designs of interior decoration have long been considered elegant and refined. Many of the French styles are named for the political period in which they appeared, therefore, much of the furniture carried the name of the king or queen who reigned during that period.

Baroque

The decor of Louis XIV (1643-1715) was grand and massive, designed for palaces and castles. It was heavy and masculine with ornate and lavish **embellishments** of animal forms, nature, and mythology. Costly decorations including **marquetry** with tortoise shell, ivory, pearls, and brass **veneers** were used; these had originated in Italy in the tenth century. The use of **gilt**, strong colors, and velvet fabric with oversized patterns were other examples of this period. **Tapestries** were used as a backdrop to throne-like chairs. The style of the day was known as **baroque**.

Louis XV chair

During the reign of Louis XV (1715-1774), the aristocrats moved into the city (Paris) apartments. Therefore, the designers began making small and intimate furniture styles that would fit better in these smaller accommodations. The aristocrats wanted elaborate design so that their prestige and riches would still be exemplified. The style of the period was known as **rococo**. Rococo's distinct attribute was the rejection of classical **motif** in favor of those based on asymmetrical arrangements of shells, rocks, flowers and vegetation, scrolls and curves. Interior decorators often papered or painted the walls during this period with elaborate floral patterns in pastel shades of pinks, greens, and gold. A feature of the furniture of this period were carved curved-line decorations. One example that is still popular today is the "cabriole," which is when the leg of the table or chair is carved with an out-curved

Cabriole leg

3

Neoclassic table

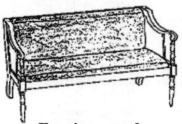

Empire couch

French Provincial

Panetiere

Pennsylvania Dutch

knee and an in-curved ankle in the shape of an inverted S-curve. It usually terminated in what resembled the foot of an animal. The **chaise lounge** was also developed at this time.

During the reign of Louis XVI (1774-1792), the ancient Roman city of Pompeii was excavated. This inspired an interest in Greek and Roman furnishings. Patterns became simplified and geometric. Curves were straightened out (straight legs) and lines became more slender and delicate with an emphasis on vertical lines (rectangular forms). **Fluting** was used for decorative accent. Because of the revival of the Greek and Roman influence in the furniture and artwork, this period became known as **neoclassic**. It carried right into the Empire period.

Napoleon reigned during the Empire period (1804-1815). He tried to turn Paris into a replica of ancient Rome. Decorative features from Egypt, Crete, Greece, and Rome entered the repertoire of Napoleonic craftsmen. The best examples of the neoclassic design of the Empire period in interior decorations can be found in the table legs which were copies of Greek and Roman temple columns. Greek **sphinxes** were used for arms of chairs, and classical scrolls were used for chair backs.

French Provincial furniture originated in the provinces of France rather than in the capital, Paris. Although the French Provincial furniture has some of the elegance of the Paris furniture it imitated, it is cruder in proportion. Some Provincial pieces were made to fulfill a specific need of the villager that was not needed in the Paris apartment. One example of furniture that was made in Provincial style and in no other, is the **panetiere**, a cabinet for storing bread. The French Provincial style of furniture is still quite popular today whether it is an original antique or a modern reproduction.

Germanic Countries. Germany was made up of cities, villages, and land joined only by a common language until the end of the nineteenth century. Until then there was no governing body or central authority to influence art and decorative design. German kings, dukes, and counts looked to Paris for their palace decorations, and the peasants designed their own decorations.

German peasant designs were characterized by geometric shapes, usually angular and heavy, and were evidenced in the cut of the furniture. Even the designs painted on the furniture, such as birds and flowers, were flat geometric forms. This style, however, creates a cozy, warm atmosphere. The German peasant style influenced the Pennsylvania Dutch of America.

The Biedermeier style of furniture was named after Father Biedermeier, who was a solid German citizen with a large family. Humorous poems were written about his middle-class values and way of life. The Biedermeier style is a neutral, practical style of furniture fashioned after the Empire decorations of France and qualities of the German peasant furniture. It is the middle-class form of the Empire style.

Biedermeier table

Spain. Spanish furniture was influenced by the Moors, Renaissance craftsmen, and practicality. Since the Islamic religion forbids the use of human or animal forms in its art, the decorations were plain and had a strong sense of geometric pattern. The Renaissance craftsmen produced heavily proportioned furniture in which line dominated over surface decoration. The Spanish used wood salvaged from their ships to make furniture. The Spanish style of furniture has a feeling of weight, mass, and color; it is solid and dark. The Spanish designers were the first to use *wainscot*, which is wood or tile paneling reaching partway up a wall. For decades, Spanish interior decoration has been adapted in homes in the southwestern United States and California.

Spanish chair

Answer the following.

1.1 Explain the difference between furniture from the reigns of Louis XIV and Louis XV. What caused this change to come about?

_____

_____

1.2 What historical event influenced the furniture style during the reign of Louis XVI?

_____

_____

1.3 How did French Provincial styles differ from their Parisian counterparts?

_____

_____

1.4 Pennsylvania Dutch furniture was crafted by whom? Briefly describe their work.

_____

_____

1.5 What three things influenced Spanish-style furniture?

a. _____

b. _____

c. _____

1.6 Describe several characteristics of Spanish-style furniture.

_____

_____

5

1.7 _____ fluting   a. Louis XIV

1.8 _____ panetiere   b. Louis XV

1.9 _____ Cabriole leg   c. Louis XVI

1.10 _____ wainscot   d. Napoleon

1.11 _____ baroque   e. Provincial

1.12 _____ Pennsylvania Dutch   f. German peasant

1.13 _____ Empire   g. Biedermeier

1.14 _____ neutral style   h. Spanish

ENGLISH DESIGN

Early English (before 1750). Historical events and explorations, changing culture, and strong personalities and preferences influenced the English design just as it had on the continent. Just as the continental styles influenced the English design, the English designs were highly influential to other parts of the world, especially the British colonies.

Tudor-style table

Tudor, Elizabethan, Jacobean, and William and Mary are names of English styles in the sixteenth and seventeenth centuries. They are the names of families and monarchs who ruled during this time. It is the period of time of the English colonization of the Eastern seaboard of the United States. Houses of this time period were built "half-timbered"; the spaces between the heavy wood supports of the building were filled with **stucco**. They had heavy beamed ceilings and dark wood paneling. Furniture was built for strength and practicality. Table legs were thick and chair backs were heavy. Grinling Gibbons was a wood carver in England at the end of the seventeenth century. He carved heavy intricate decorations into wood that was used for paneling, fireplace mantel decorations, and frames of paintings and mirrors.

Queen Anne (early 18th century). Queen Anne is applied to the interior decorations of the early eighteenth century, coinciding with Louis XV in France. Again, the aristocrats wanted the same elaborate royal designs as used in their estates only scaled down for the smaller rooms of their city apartments. The furniture had many curved lines but was considerably more simple because ornate carving was abandoned. The English designers borrowed the cabriole chair leg from the French; however, the chair leg was redesigned to terminate in a "claw and ball." This was a table, desk, or chair leg carved as the foot of an animal grasping a ball in its claws.

Claw and ball

Chippendale chair

Windsor chair

In the Queen Anne period, two types of furniture styles appeared that are still popular today. The Windsor chair has curved lines and is informal in appearance. It has a curved back and arms for a comfortable fit.

The other furniture style that appeared in the late eighteenth century (the end of the Queen Anne period) was designed by a father and son, both named Thomas Chippendale. They adapted many of the designs of the period and borrowed heavily from French Louis XV rococo designs. They used curving lines and elaborate decorations and incorporated Chinese motifs in their decorations.

Neoclassic or Georgian. Once again, the period from 1750 to 1820 was known as the "neoclassic" period because of the excavation of the ancient Roman city of Pompeii. The English furniture design of this time period was know as "Georgian" after the kings George I through IV. Furniture was designed in enormous scale with dramatic colors, gilded surfaces, and marble tabletops. The great lion-paw feet persisted. Veneer and **inlay** replaced carving as the dominant decoration, and straight legs replaced the cabriole leg.

Hepplewhite chair

Sheraton dresser

The Adams brothers became famous for copies of interior decorations found in the excavations of Pompeii. They designed a fireplace mantel that was supported by temple columns, and the Greek vase shapes were prevalent in their decorations.

Both George Hepplewhite and Thomas Sheraton were furniture designers of this time as well. Hepplewhite used simple, graceful lines and distinct chair backs. The shield-back chair is associated with Hepplewhite, as is the painted motif of feathers and wheat occasionally found on the back. Sheraton used more straight lines. The Sheraton chairs generally have a rectangular or shield-back with an urn or lyre-shaped **splats**.

Victorian-style bead lamps

Victorian (1837-1901). The Victorian period of English design suffered greatly. Historical reasons explain the particular lack of taste of this period. The Industrial Revolution made it possible to manufacture furniture by machine, cheapening the quality of workmanship. With this ability to make furniture by machine came new materials; applied ornamentation out of metal and wood replaced carved designs. Since Queen Victoria was a puritanical person, as was the society she ruled, sentimentality ruled interior decor during this period. Sweetness, prettiness, and picturesqueness replaced the restrained taste and simple-but-sturdy proportions of earlier periods. These are not good design principles for interior decorations. The Victorian designers attempted to borrow designs from various time eras and used them together. This borrowing of ideas is called **eclecticism**.

The results of Victorian design were often confusing, lacking in taste, cluttered, used a variety of styles, and left no place in the room where you could rest.

Answer the following.

1.15   Define "half-timbered."

_____

_____

1.16   What feature did the Queen Anne-style furniture borrow from the French? _____

How did they change it? _____

1.17   Describe a Windsor chair.

_____

1.18   What kind of motif did Chippendales incorporate into their design?

_____

1.19   List three designers that contributed to the neoclassic style of English design.

a. _____

b. _____

c. _____

1.20   List several features that are shared by both Hepplewhite and Sheraton styles.

_____

_____

1.21   Describe the Hepplewhite chair back style.

_____

1.22   What influence did the Industrial Revolution have on interior decorating and the furniture produced in this period?

_____

_____

_____

1.23   Define *eclecticism*.

_____

_____

TRADITIONAL AMERICAN DESIGN

Drop leaf table

All styles of furniture made during the colonial and early national periods of America ultimately derived from European sources. They were usually taken from the lesser gentry, not the elaborate costly furniture made for royalty and the aristocrats.

American furniture displays regional differences and ethnic diversity. For example, Massachusetts and Rhode Island derived their furniture styles from the English. Pennsylvania was settled by German-speaking countries so their furniture styles derived from the Germans and Dutch. Spain was a major influence on the styles in the Southwest and the French in the Mississippi Valley.

Early American. The first settlers to America faced vast areas of pine forests. Since they had to clear many of these trees in order to make room to build homesteads, it is only logical that most of their homes and furnishings were made of pine wood. Most of their designs were based on the William and Mary style which is what the baroque style is known as today. The early American designs were more simple and less decorative, however. They were extremely practical and space saving. Examples of some of the space-saving furniture are the drop-leaf table, table/chair combination, and the storage chest benches.

In general, the Early American design can be described as the seventeenth English provincial style. Because most early settlers had only furniture for home decoration, any other decorations were practical. They included pewter bowls and mugs or the copper and iron cooking utensils for the kitchen. Overall, the early American designs created a cozy, informal atmosphere.

Georgian (colonial). A few generations after the first settlers had come to America, bigger and more refined homes were built in the towns that had replaced the villages. This period is referred to as "colonial" and corresponds to the reigns of King George I, II, and III of England. The Queen Anne style was the true inspiration for America interior decoration. In 1754 Chippendale published a book of furniture, so the craftsmen no longer had to rely on memory for furniture making. The first rocking chair, truly an American piece of furniture, was invented by a Shaker craftsman. It was called the Boston rocker because it originated in New England.

Federal "neoclassic." By the time the American Revolution had been fought and won, a new decorative design had appeared in Europe; the "neoclassic" designs of the Adams Brothers, Hepplewhite, and Sheraton. It was called "federal" style in America because it was the style of the new federation of states known as the United States. This style continued well into the nineteenth century.

Duncan Phyfe chair

Duncan Phyfe is the most well known name in American furniture. His designs followed the same simple lines as Sheraton; table legs, chair backs, and sofa arms had gentle curves and the legs often ended in animal feet. He used rosettes, lyre shapes, **cornucopias,** and garlands to decorate his furniture pieces.

Hitchcock chairs

Another furniture designer of the federal period was Lambert Hitchcock. He is best known for his uniquely styled chair. His chairs were made completely of wood, though sometimes they had a cane seat. The unique quality of his chairs was the finish he gave them. They were painted black with gold stenciling. The stenciling was of patriotic symbols or of a country motif.

Shakers. The Shakers were a religious sect that flourished in the nineteenth century. They had fled to America from England because of religious persecution. They lived in communes in New York, Connecticut, Massachusetts, and Kentucky. They based their furniture on the Early colonial styles of American furniture; function and simplicity were stressed. The natural wood grain was emphasized, not stained or lacquered, and it was void of embellishments. The unique contributions of the Shakers were the built-in cupboards and dressers, cot-like beds on rollers, and the cast-iron stove.

Shaker chair

Victorian America (1840-1900) "sentimentalism." Many of the classic ideas in decorations were replaced by this "new" style of imitations of Gothic and Renaissance designs. The American Victorian period was more forbidding than the English, due to its use of dark colors. To avoid clutter, modern designers recommend using individual items from Victorian decoration as a single furnishing in a modern room rather than decorating an entire room or home with it.

Answer the following.

1.24   List several features of Early American furniture.

_____

1.25   Give two examples of space-saving furniture.

    a. _____

    b. _____

1.26   What are two examples of practical decorations Early Americans would have used?

_____

1.27   In the United States, the Federal style included the designs of which four Englishmen?

_____

1.28   Who was the most famous American furniture maker? _____

1.29   List several characteristics of his designs.

_____

_____

1.30   What was unique about a Hitchcock chair?

_____

_____

1.31   Who were the Shakers? _____

_____

_____

1.32   Describe the Shaker furniture style.

_____

_____

1.33   List two of their unique contributions.

        a. _____

        b. _____

1.34   How did the Victorian style of America differ from the same style in England?

_____

_____

TWENTIETH-CENTURY DESIGN

It became apparent to designers that the Victorian period produced furniture of lesser quality made from unoriginal designs. Most designs were poor reproductions of the well-crafted pieces made before the industrial revolution. Instead of trying to recreate the beauty of hand-carved furniture, twentieth-century designers developed new designs suitable for machine production.

Twentieth-century artistic designers created original designs which reflected their time, letting materials and technology guide them toward their goal. Their creations reflect many of the ideas of modern art and are international in spirit.

We will begin at the first of the century and examine some of the movements in design and some of the important contributions made by designers of different countries.

Tiffany lamp reproduction

Art Nouveau. The Art Nouveau style was inspired from the paintings of French artists such as Gauguin and Toulouse-Lautrec. It literally translates as "new art." It was characterized by flowing lines of plant forms. The leading name in European Art Nouveau was Henry van de Velde who designed fabric, lamps, and furniture. In America, Louis Tiffany led the way by creating lamps, vases, and stained glass windows.

The Bauhaus. The Bauhaus was originally a school of art in Germany that believed in mass production and economy of materials, which incorporated designs for that purpose. The Bauhaus movement was dedicated to the idea that "form follows function." Marcel Breuer studied at the school and stayed on as an instructor in the machine shop of the school. He designed a tubular steel chair to be produced by machine. Today, we might see examples of Breuer's designs in office and lawn furniture.

Tubular chair, 1930s

International Style. When the Nazis came to power in Germany, they closed the Bauhaus school. As a result, many of its members immigrated to the U. S. Their creative ideas soon influenced American home furnishing and architecture. Ludwig Mies van der Rohe was the director of the Bauhaus before the Nazis closed it. In America he was famous for his architectural skills; he designed skyscrapers in Chicago. He is known for his influence in promoting the international style where the catch phrase was "less is more." The chair (the bent-steel chair) he designed joined that of Marcel Breuer to become one of the most influential products of the German Bauhaus.

A room by Raymond Loewy, 1934

Art Deco. This style was named after the *Exposition Internatiaonale des Arts Decoratifs*, which was held in Paris in 1925. It is a modernistic style characterized by bold outlines, streamline forms, zigzags, and patterns suggestive of modern machinery. The Chrysler Building and Radio City Music Hall in New York City are great examples of Art Deco architecture. Furniture, paintings, and glassware were also created in this style.

Scandinavian designs. Scandinavian designs of the twentieth century were machine-crafted. Simplicity of design is the characteristic of this group. Alvar Aalto from Finland created a bent plywood chair.

12

Italian Design. The Italians since the 1960s have brought great improvement and refinements to "modular furniture." Modular furniture is furniture with individual units that may be interchanged to make different arrangements. Modular furniture is used in doctors' offices and schools where versatility of movable, interlocking chairs is important.

American Design. Since World War II, America has been a leader in the creation of modern home designs. Eero Saarinen, a famous American architect, designed a plastic shell chair. He did away with chair and table legs and designed a single pedestal base cast in plastic.

Bent plywood chair

Charles Eames designed molded plywood and metal furniture. His plastic chair, designed in 1941, is still popular today. It's another great example of using new materials for durable, streamlined furniture.

Of course, the computer age has required furniture designers to create special furniture for the home as well as the office for computer equipment.

There has been a revival of Early American design. The country style so popular today is an attempt to recall the homier, old-fashioned look of times gone by.

It will be interesting to see what the twenty-first century architects and interior designers will create for the future.

Answer the following.

1.35   What does *Art Nouveau* mean? _____

1.36   Who led the Art Nouveau movement in the United States? _____

1.37   What are his best-known works?_____

_____

1.38   Marcel Breuer was famous for what style of construction?_____

_____

1.39   List several furniture pieces in which we might see Breuer's ideas today.

_____

_____

1.40   Who was the leader of the International style who coined the phrase "less is more"?

_____

1.41   In what city did Art Deco originate? _____

1.42   What two famous buildings in New York City represent Art Deco architectural style?

_____

1.43   Who created the Scandinavian-designed bent plywood chair?

_____

1.44   Modular furniture is associated with what country's designers?

_____

1.45   What designer created the single pedestal base for chairs and tables?

_____

Complete the activity.

1.46   For this activity, you will need 15 3″ x 5″ cards. Label each card with the time periods listed below. Cut out pictures of furniture from decorating magazines, catalogs, and furniture sale ads, and glue them on the appropriate card. Explain why you think each piece of furniture belongs in the time period you have assigned it. What characteristics does it have that identifies it as belonging to this time period?

<table>
<tr><td>Louis XV or Louis XVI</td><td>French Provincial</td></tr>
<tr><td>Pennsylvania Dutch</td><td>Spanish</td></tr>
<tr><td>Queen Anne</td><td>Windsor chair</td></tr>
<tr><td>Chippendale</td><td>Hepplewhite</td></tr>
<tr><td>Sheraton</td><td>Victorian</td></tr>
<tr><td>Hitchcock chair</td><td>Duncan Phyfe</td></tr>
<tr><td>Shaker</td><td>Federal</td></tr>
<tr><td>an Early American room</td><td></td></tr>
</table>

Example:

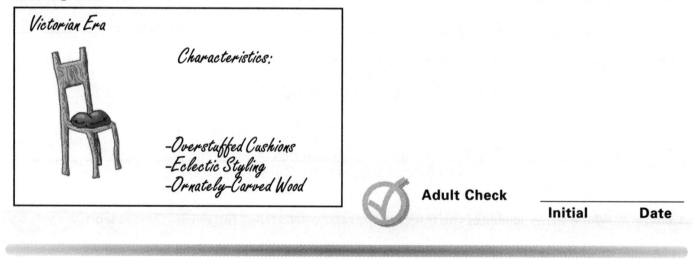

Victorian Era

Characteristics:

-Overstuffed Cushions
-Eclectic Styling
-Ornately-Carved Wood

Adult Check _____
                  Initial   Date

Review the material in this section in preparation for the Self Test. The Self Test will check your mastery of this particular section. The items missed on this Self Test will indicate specific areas where restudy is needed for mastery.

SELF TEST 1

Write the correct word in the appropriate space (each answer, 4 points).

Breuer	Duncan Phyfe
Federal	German peasants
Hepplewhite	Hitchcock
Louis XIV	Louis XV
Napoleon	Shakers

1.01   During the reign of _____ the decor was grand and massive and the ornate and lavish style of the day was baroque.

1.02   During the 18th century _____'s reign developed a rococo style with flowing serpentine curves.

1.03   The decorative style known as *Empire* refers to the French Empire of _____ .

1.04   Pennsylvania Dutch furniture was crafted by _____ .

1.05   _____ is best known for the shield back chair.

1.06   _____ is noted for use of lyre motif, cornucopia legs, and pedestal bases.

1.07   The _____ made furniture that was simple, using straight lines and no stain or lacquer.

1.08   A _____ chair would be painted black with gold-stenciled decoration.

1.09   The _____ style of furniture was the result of the American Revolution.

1.010   _____ designed a chair of tubular construction.

Answer *true* **or** *false* (each answer, 4 points).

1.011   _____   Biedermeier is the name of a famous German furniture designer.

1.012   _____   The first rocking chair was designed by Windsor.

1.013   _____   Duncan Phyfe was the most famous American furniture maker.

1.014   _____   Chippendale is known for curving lines and Chinese motifs.

1.015   _____   Louis Tiffany led the Art Nouveau movement in the U.S.

Answer the following (each answer, 5 points).

1.016   What historical event influenced the furniture style during the reign of Louis XVI?

_____

_____

15

1.017   What is *wainscot* and what style of interior uses it often?

_____

_____

1.018   What feature did the Queen Anne-style furniture borrow from the French?

_____

_____

1.019   List the four designers who contributed to the "neoclassic" style.

_____

_____

1.020   Define *eclecticism*.

_____

1.021   Give two examples of space-saving furniture.

_____

_____

1.022   How did the Victorian style in America differ from the same style in England?

_____

_____

Essay Question (answer, 5 points).

1.023   What influence did the Industrial Revolution have on interior decorating and the furniture produced in this period?

_____

_____

_____

_____

Score   _____

Adult Check   _____

                                    Initial   Date

II. INTRODUCTION TO DESIGN AND DECORATION

The term *interior decoration* was used for fifty years before the term "interior design" became known. For our purposes here we will use the term "interior design" because it reflects what this study is about. It implies the necessity of a plan, scheme, or design that greatly influences the end result.

Interior design implies a blend of ideas, reasoning, planning, and taste. When a designer chooses a room to decorate, he or she must consider two things: the function of the room and personal preferences or tastes. The function of the room is probably a matter of fact—"this is a bedroom," or "this is a dining room." Personal preferences or tastes are what make the room your own. Things to consider include whether you want the room to be formal or informal, bright or subdued, and what colors should be used.

The elements of design—color, line, texture, form, and space—are all major points to consider in decorating. Also important to your overall decorating scheme are the six principles of design: proportion, scale, balance, rhythm, emphasis, and unity. By using these principles along with the elements of design, you can achieve a very pleasing result.

Before you are ready to start remodeling or designing a room there are some basic decorating techniques that must be learned. These will also be discussed in this section.

Section Objectives

Review these objectives. When you have completed this section, you should be able to:

4. Explain the elements and principles of design as they pertain to interior decoration.

5. Gain skills in practical techniques of interior decoration.

6. Learn the basics of furniture arrangement from room to room.

ELEMENTS AND PRINCIPLES OF DESIGN

Although elements and principles of design were covered in LIFEPAC 4, a short review will be given here. It is important to learn how the elements and principles of design come into play in interior design.

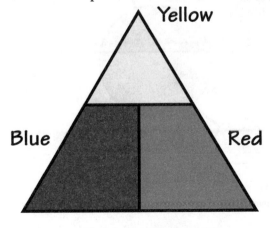

Primary Colors

Color is the most important, versatile, and distinctive element of design. It can transform a home more quickly and cheaply than any other decorative device, disguising faults and altering the feeling of a space in as short a time as it takes to paint or cover the walls. Color is almost always the first thing you notice when you enter a room.

The primary colors are red, blue, and yellow. All other colors are made from these three colors.

By mixing equal amounts of red and blue, we get the color purple; by mixing equal amounts of blue and yellow, we get the color green; by mixing equal amounts of red and yellow, we get the color orange. Purple, green, and orange are called secondary colors.

In order to complete the color wheel, we combine an equal amount of each primary color to its adjacent secondary color to form an intermediate color. Usually the primary color is listed first; blue-purple, red-orange, yellow-green. Complementary colors are colors opposite each other on the color wheel.

Hue is simply the name of the color. In the color spectrum, each color name basically distinguishes it from another. Each hue can have a large range of values; the red hue, for example, can have a value range from pink to maroon. Remember *value* is the lightness or darkness of color. Value indicates how dark any given hue is, on a value scale with black being the darkest and white being the lightest. Actually, black and white are not true colors. White represents pure light and black represents the total absence of light.

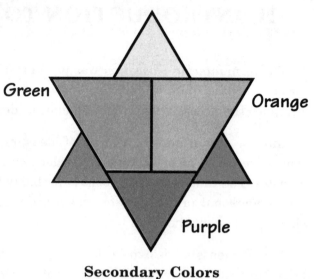

Secondary Colors

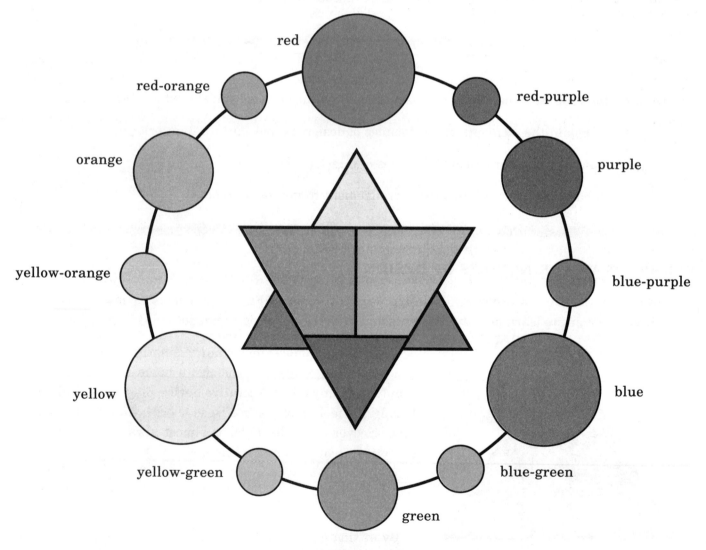

The Color Wheel

18

A hue combined with black is called a *shade*. Examples of shades: red + black = maroon, orange + black = brown, yellow + black = gold, blue + black = navy, and purple + black = violet.

A hue combined with white is called a tint. Examples of tints: red + white = pink, orange + white = peach, yellow + white = ivory, purple + white = lavender.

Another way to change a color is to add gray to the original hue, producing a tone. Adding gray to a color makes it more subdued.

Values of color can be used to change the appearance of the room. It can be used to create optical illusions. By using light values, you can make a room look larger. Conversely, dark values make a room appear smaller.

Intensity is how bright or dull a color is—the measure of a color's strength or grayness. The color wheel is composed of twelve colors in their brightest or fullest intensity. You can subdue these colors by adding black, white, gray, or a complementary color to them. In interior design, background colors (walls, ceilings, and floors) are usually grayed or neutralized, because softer intensities are much easier on the eye.

If you divide the color wheel in half, one side makes up the "warm" colors and the other half would be composed of "cool" colors. Warm colors are red, orange, and yellow; so called because they are analogous to fire, heat, and sun. The cool colors are green, blue, and purple; so called because they often represent fields, sky, and water. Colors reflect mood. Warm colors seem to be cheerful and inviting, while cool colors seem more restful.

Value and intensity affects the look of a room. Warm colors are the "advancing" colors and make an object appear closer. Cool colors are "receding" colors. In other words, a wall painted yellow will appear closer than a wall painted blue. When a bright color is used against a background of a subdued color, the bright color will stand out more. A closet door painted bright blue will definitely stand out when the rest of the room is painted a soft lavender.

When a dark color is used against a subdued background, the dark color will advance. A wall painted navy blue will seem closer than a wall painted a soft, muted green. You can see how this can change the appearance of the proportion of a room. An extra long room can appear shorter if one end wall is painted a darker or brighter color. In a square room, any one wall or two opposite walls could be painted a more advancing color to make the room look better proportioned.

From a decorator's point of view, the best proportion for a room is a 2:3 proportion. That occurs when the sides of the room are one-and-a-half times the length of the ends of the room.

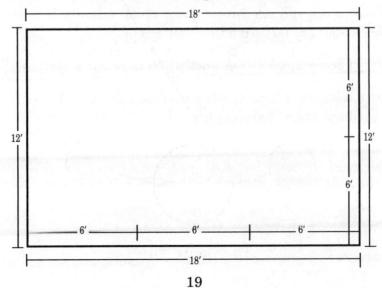

Since not all rooms are perfectly proportioned, besides color the designer must use texture, line, form, and space to give the illusion of good proportion. These will be looked at more closely later in this section when we study the principles of design.

A guideline, but not a fixed rule, for selecting and distributing colors in a room is: the ceiling should be the lightest color, the wall color should be darker than the ceiling but lighter than the floor and the floor should be the darkest.

Walls are important in the control of the color scheme you decide on. They bring all the colors of a room together. Although there are no strict rules for choosing a color scheme there are some important principles that will guide you. A room's purpose should affect the colors you choose. Light colors are best for rooms in which you plan to work: the kitchen, den, study room, etc. Light colors reflect light, which makes working easier.

Another important consideration is the location of the room. Light reflecting colors are important for rooms with a northern exposure, because these rooms get little sunlight. Likewise, light-colored rooms that get good sunlight exposure can be too bright for comfort.

Personal taste plays an important role in deciding on a color scheme. You may prefer red and a friend may prefer blue. Guidelines are good but they may not reflect your personal desires. However, don't be so excited about a color that you use it everywhere. Color contrasts are good and a room without contrasts can soon become boring.

Working out the best combination of colors or the best color scheme for a room is of prime importance. A monochromatic color scheme revolves around one basic color. One way to develop an interesting monochromatic scheme is to think about that color in depth. Take blue, for example, and think of the sky. Think of the pale blue-violet blossoms of the blue phlox or pansies; the blue flowers of the primrose. Think of different precious gems and stones like blue topaz, sapphire, and turquoise. Think of the **cerulean** blue of the bluebird, the brilliant blue of the blue jay, or the slate blue of the blue heron. Think about the blue-green of sea struck by sun. These natural combinations can be used to build up interesting monochromatic color schemes.

As you may remember, other types of color schemes are as follows:

analogous. the use of three hues next to each other on the color wheel

extended analogous. the use of half of the color wheel
Don't forget to vary the values and intensities to add visual interest. It is not necessary to use equal amounts of each color. Some may be used only as an accent.

complementary. the use of colors opposite one another on the color wheel

triad. the use of any three colors that form a triangle on the color wheel:
primary colors or secondary colors, for example

Complete the following activity.

2.1   Using colors at their fullest intensity, complete the color wheel, using markers or crayons.

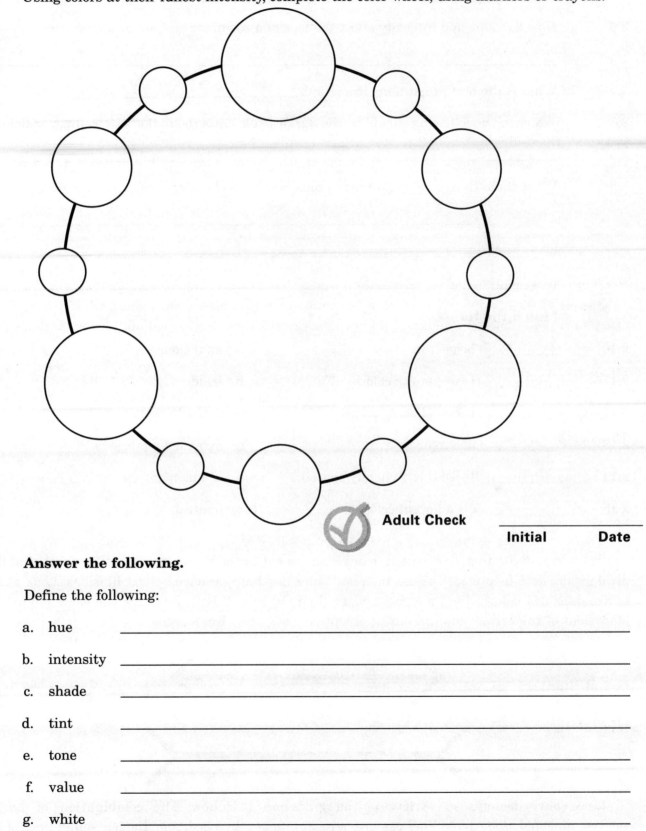

Adult Check   _____
                   Initial   Date

 Answer the following.

2.2   Define the following:

a.   hue   _____

b.   intensity   _____

c.   shade   _____

d.   tint   _____

e.   tone   _____

f.   value   _____

g.   white   _____

2.3   A color that represents fire, heat, and sun is a _____ color.

2.4   An example of a cool color is _____ .

21

2.5   How do colors create mood?

_____

2.6   How do value and intensity affect the look of a room?

_____

2.7   What is the best proportion for a room? _____

2.8   Which of the following should be the darkest color in a room; the wall, ceiling, or floor?

_____

2.9   What three things are important to consider when choosing a color scheme for a room?

        a. _____

        b. _____

        c. _____

Match the terms.

2.10   _____ beige, tan, ivory   a. analogous

2.11   _____ two opposite colors   b. triad

2.12   _____ three adjacent colors   c. monochromatic

2.13   _____ one color   d. extended analogous

2.14   _____ three colors equally spaced   e. complementary

2.15   _____ six adjacent colors   f. neutral

In interior decorating, *line* is used to describe the outline of a form or shape. The purpose of line is to divide space and help create visual interest. Lines can help produce optical illusions. Look at the two horizontal lines below. Does one look longer than the other? Both lines are the same length, but the placement of the arrows changes our perception of the line lengths.

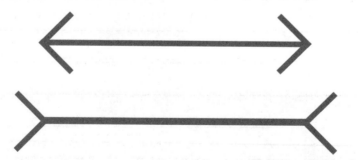

Lines convey feelings so variety is the guideline to follow. The combination of horizontal, vertical, diagonal, and curved lines can give a room interest. In a bedroom, the horizontal lines of the bed, desk, and night stand creates a feeling of repose. Drapes with their vertical folds add formality. The walls, doorway, and windows combine these two main lines. Curved and diagonal lines add diversity and can be seen in table and chair legs, pillows, lamps, and knickknacks.

Types of Lines and Their Effects

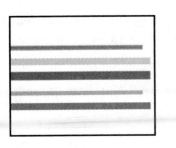

Horizontal Lines—repose, security

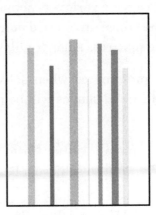

Vertical Lines—strength, dignity

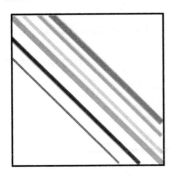

Diagonal Lines—action, movement

Curved Lines—gentleness, quiet, restfulness

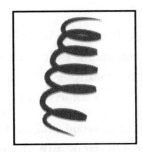

Tight Curves—springiness

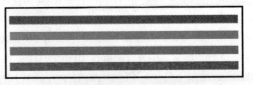

Delicate, Fine Lines—daintiness

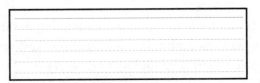

Heavy Lines—boldness

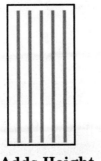

Adds Height

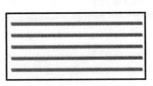

Adds Width

23

Combining lines gives an object shape or "form." Furniture designers work with three-dimensional materials to create a wide variety of shapes. A bed, for example, is made with both horizontal and vertical lines. The horizontal lines are more dominant, creating a feeling of repose. Curved lines may also be seen in the shape of the mattress edge or pillows.

Everyone has preferences when selecting the lines for a room. If a more feminine appearance is desired, the use of curved shapes will be predominant. For a more masculine or tailored room, straighter lines are used.

Everything in a room is either "form" or "space." **Space** is a three-dimensional setting for furniture and furnishings. We want to achieve a balance between these two elements of design.

In decorating we often try to create an illusion of space. The following techniques can help create this effect.

- ✔ light colors on the walls (giving a receding effect)
- ✔ wall-to-wall carpet
- ✔ large doors and windows (encouraging the eye to travel beyond the space of the room)
- ✔ furniture in scale with the room (The furniture designed for the Paris apartments was a smaller version of the elaborate, massive furniture designed for castles and palaces.)
- ✔ similar colors for walls, carpet, and furniture
- ✔ rooms with an open plan that have the same carpeting extending to the next room
- ✔ background materials that do not distract the eye
- ✔ mirrors

Texture refers to the surface covering of fabrics, furniture, and furnishings. It appeals to the sense of touch as well as sight. It adds interest and variety to the overall effect of the room. Colors can be so radically changed or modified by cleverly used texture and pattern that through its subtlety of finish even a one-color room can be made to look just as lively and interesting as a more vividly colored one.

Texture can change the character of a room. Different flooring materials, such as wood, tile, and carpet create different impressions. Some textures are compatible while others may clash. **Brocade** and **chintz** furniture upholstery material would not look good together in the same room. Why? Because brocade is an expensive fabric with a raised decorative pattern, while chintz is an inexpensive cotton material printed with several colors. Texture, then, can also determine whether a room is formal or informal.

Answer the following.

2.16   What is *line* used for in interior decorating?

_____

2.17   Identify two pieces of furniture that utilize a horizontal line.

_____

2.18   Identify two pieces of furniture that utilize a vertical line.

_____

Match—answers may be used more than once.

2.19	_____ repose, security	a.	curved lines
2.20	_____ action, movement	b.	delicate, fine lines
2.21	_____ springiness	c.	diagonal lines
2.22	_____ strength, dignity	d.	heavy lines
2.23	_____ daintiness	e.	horizontal lines
2.24	_____ adds width	f.	tight curved lines
2.25	_____ adds height	g.	vertical lines
2.26	_____ gentleness, quiet		
2.27	_____ boldness		

2.28   Define space.

_____

2.29   Define texture.

_____

Answer *true* **or** *false*.

2.30   _____ You can mix and match any textures to create variety and interest in a room.

The principles of design show how to make the best use of space, whether by structural or decorative means; how to choose appropriate lighting and color schemes; how to go about mixing texture and pattern.

Proportion is a pleasing relationship among all parts, resulting in harmony of the design as a whole. It refers to the division of space created by the value and intensity of the colors, between the quality and kinds of textures, line, form, and space. This principle can be applied to the furniture itself or to the furniture when compared with its surroundings. For example, look at the two chairs on the right; which chair has legs that seem sturdy enough to hold the weight of that chair?

Look at the table lamps below. Are the shades in good proportion to the base?

Which lamp has the best proportion?

As a general rule, rooms will appear large if light and neutral-colored objects are used in larger proportion than bright colors. Using an uneven distribution of any element will be more interesting than equal divisions. It is easier to decorate a room with a 2:3 proportion than a room that is square.

Scale is the size of the parts of a design or a group of objects in comparison to each other. Scale is also related to people and their use of an object. Small furniture fits best in a small room. Using large, bulky furniture in a small room makes the room appear smaller. A large chair at a small desk or a small, low chair at a large dining table are out of scale. Furniture should also fit the body. A large, overstuffed chair would be out of scale with a small person, as a small desk chair would be out of scale with a large person.

Balance in design creates a pleasing effect. It makes things appear that they belong where they are. There are two types of balance: symmetrical and asymmetrical. Symmetrical balance (where one side matches the other), is also known as formal balance. Asymmetrical is more informal and is where the two halves of the arrangement are not the same, but are still balanced.

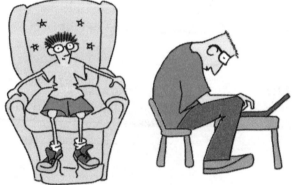

Asymmetrical balance is more challenging, but it is also more interesting. It can be achieved in several ways. Since darker-colored objects appear heavier than lighter-colored objects, you may be able to use a larger, light-colored object to balance a small, darker one. Another way to achieve asymmetrical balance is to use several smaller objects to balance one larger object.

Rhythm allows the eye to move from one part of a design to other areas. In order for the effect to be pleasing, the movement should be smooth. Rhythm can be created by repeating a color, design, line, or shape in several areas of the room, by varying the size of the shapes or lines in a sequence, or by using a progression of tints or shades of a color. See how your eye moves with the rhythm produced by the two examples below.

Emphasis is stress placed on what is important. It draws attention to the **focal point** (or point of interest) of the room. The focal point can be a large picture, a brightly patterned rug, a piece of furniture, or an architectural structure like a fireplace or a bay window. A room where nothing catches your eye is boring. Every room should have a focal point, but too many focal points or areas of interest can be confusing and detract from the good design of a room.

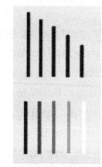

Unity is the harmonious effect achieved by the good use of the elements and principles of design. It is the overall effect created by the entire room.

Answer the following.

2.31   Define proportion.

_____

_____

2.32   Define scale.

_____

_____

2.33   Large furniture in a small room is an example of a room with poor _____ .

2.34   Symmetrical balance is also known as _____ balance.

2.35   Give an example of how you can achieve the effect of asymmetrical balance.

_____

_____

2.36   List three ways to create rhythm in a room.

a.   _____

b.   _____

c.   _____

2.37   Define focal point.

_____

_____

PRACTICAL TECHNIQUES OF INTERIOR DESIGN

Interior design has some practical techniques that make the job of redecorating a room or just rearranging furniture in an existing room much easier. The first tool to be mastered is the floor plan. A floor plan is a scale drawing showing length and width of a room or rooms.

Furniture can be rearranged by simply moving it until you get the desired look or effect. However, the use of a floor plan is less physically straining and less damaging to furniture and possibly walls. It is the practical way.

Just as a writer needs an outline for structure and unity in a paper or a book, the decorator makes a floor plan for a room to be decorated in order to prepare the details for that room in advance. It is essential for a successful and pleasing result.

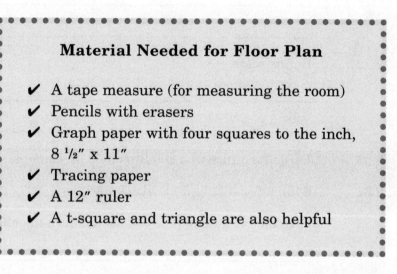

Material Needed for Floor Plan

✔ A tape measure (for measuring the room)
✔ Pencils with erasers
✔ Graph paper with four squares to the inch, 8 ½" x 11"
✔ Tracing paper
✔ A 12" ruler
✔ A t-square and triangle are also helpful

Since you will be formulating a plan for redecorating your bedroom, you will need to use it as the subject for making a floor plan.

Complete the following activity. Put a check in each box upon completion.

2.38 ☐ Measure the width and length of your bedroom room and then convert the measurements in feet to measurements for the floor plan. The scale is ¼" = 1'. So, one square on your graph paper will equal one foot of your bedroom wall. Four squares on your graph paper represent four feet of wall space in your bedroom. Draw this floor plan on a sheet of graph paper.

2.39 ☐ Using the Floor Plan Symbols given, show where the doors, walls, and window(s) are in your bedroom. Be sure to measure distances in your room (such as from the windows to the corner) very carefully. Don't forget to show where the closet is located and what kind of doors it has (louver, sliding or regular door). When you have completed an accurate floor plan, use tracing paper to make several copies of it. Place all copies into an interior design loose-leaf notebook.

*Enlarged template of floor plan symbols may be found on page 69.

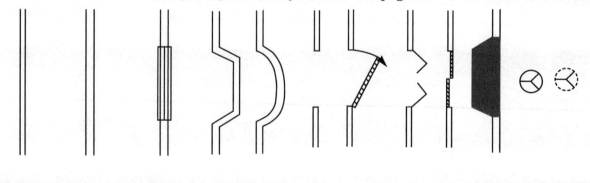

Adult Check _____
          Initial   Date

Templates are paper scale models of furniture, to use on floor plans to try various arrangements and to determine the number of different pieces and the size of furniture that your room will **accommodate**. Bedroom furniture templates are provided in this book on a scale of ¼″ = 1′.

 Complete the following activities. Put a check in each box upon completion.

2.40 ☐ Use magazines and furniture catalogs to select pictures of the pieces of furniture you will be arranging on the floor plan of your bedroom. It can be either the furniture you already possess or the furniture you want to replace (or pretend that you are replacing) for this assignment.

Select carefully, keeping in mind the guidelines of the elements and principles of design. Cut out the pictures of the selected furniture pieces and glue them to a piece of white 8 ½″ x 11″ paper to be placed in your interior design notebook.

2.41 ☐ Select and cut out the appropriate templates that represent the furniture you have or want to have for your bedroom. Prepare an envelope or a zippered plastic sandwich bag to store your templates in when you are not using them.

*Templates for cutting out can be found on pages 67–69.

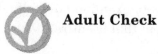 **Adult Check** _____

                                             Initial   **Date**

When an architect designs a room or rooms, he has to follow certain guidelines or rules in order to make the whole house more livable. It is important to know some of the standard rules that architects use, not only if we would wish to create a brand-new room, but also to help us to understand the existing room we have chosen to decorate. Here are some of these standard rules:

✔ Doors should swing into rooms.
✔ Less space is wasted if the door is near the corner of the room and swings into the corner.
✔ In the house as a whole, all doors—entrance, closet, bathroom—should be grouped together to conserve wall space when possible.
✔ Bedrooms should be planned to have the maximum amount of wall space.
✔ Windows in a bedroom are generally higher on the wall than they are in other rooms to allow space for furniture underneath and to provide more privacy.

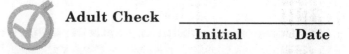

Complete the following activity. Put a check in the box upon completion.

2.42 ☐ Take a look at your room and see if it conforms to the rules on the previous page. Identify the good points and the bad points of your room. Write these down and place them in your interior design notebook. As you continue through this LIFEPAC, you should be able to find ways to improve your room through the techniques and special treatments discussed.

Adult Check _____

Initial   Date

Most houses are designed by architects with each room having a certain function. For example, a kitchen or bathroom will probably always have the same function for the life of the house. Although some rooms can be converted for different functions, most of the time the function stays the same.

The "spirit" of a room, however, can usually be changed to suit your taste. It can be done by using the elements and principles of design as previously discussed and the "spirit" of the room can be changed by simply rearranging the furniture. The arrangement of furniture in a room also determines its "livability." A crowded, cluttered room will probably be avoided. If you have to climb over a sofa and two chairs to turn on a light, you will more than likely find another place to read your book.

The kitchen will have the same function for the life of the house.

Space does not permit us to examine how to find the best arrangement for all the major rooms in a house, so we will look at a room that is entirely yours—the bedroom. Many of the guidelines are applicable to other rooms of the house.

Ideally, each person should have his or her own bedroom, but this is not always possible, due either to size of the house or size of the family. Many houses have at least three bedrooms: one for the parents, one for the girls, and one for the boys.

Architects usually place the bedrooms of the house away from the activity centers of the home such as the kitchen and family room.

Every bedroom should have enough space for a bed, a night table, and a dresser or chest of drawers. An "average" sized bedroom has from 100 to 150 square feet, which allows for more flexibility in arranging the furniture.

Most everyone has decorated or at least rearranged the furniture in their bedroom. There are many factors to consider to achieve the best results when rearranging a room. When considering what furniture and how to arrange it, you need to identify the function of the room. The function of the bedroom is to provide a place to sleep. Therefore, you need a bed. The bedroom should also provide you with a place to store your personal items and clothing; a closet and a chest of drawers, then, are necessary. It is always nice, if room permits, to include a night stand or small table next to the bed to allow easy access to a lamp,

The bed is the focal point of the bedroom.

alarm clock, and possibly a telephone. Many people study, read, watch television, sew, do crafts, or listen to music in their bedrooms. These functions require certain equipment, furniture, or lighting and must be considered when planning the room.

The bed dominates the bedroom, therefore, it is the focal point of the room. Where you place the bed and how you decorate your bed will establish the "spirit" of your room. When placing a bed or any large piece of furniture in a room, you should leave a small amount of space between the wall and the furniture. Only shelves should go directly against the wall. The other three sides of the bed should have 18″ around them to allow for making the bed. The bed should not be placed by a window because of the possibility of a draft and also any light (street light, passing car lights, and sunrise) that might disturb your sleep.

The "traffic pattern" is important both in every room and between rooms. A traffic pattern is the walkway from the door of the room to the major pieces of furniture, the closet, and the windows. You should be able to move freely between the furniture pieces. Major traffic patterns should have a minimum of 2 ½ feet. Another concern in a bedroom is the placement of furniture that has drawers extending out. Between the chest or dresser and any other object there should be at least 3 feet of space.

Once all the furniture is arranged, it is important to consider lighting. Some rooms will have an overhead light that provides general illumination. However, it is not adequate for specific tasks like putting on makeup or reading in bed. For a bedroom, a lamp on the night stand is an essential. There should also be a light somewhere in the room that is controlled by a switch by the door. A light is also needed for use at a desk or vanity table. Walk-in closets should also have a light.

Complete the following activity. Put a check in the box upon completion.

2.43 ☐ Using the floor plans that you have drawn, arrange the furniture templates that you have selected. After making one arrangement of furniture using the templates provided, you may trace that arrangement and keep it on file. Tracing a second arrangement will provide you with two samples to compare side-by-side. You should complete at least two different arrangements. Place these samples in your interior designs notebook.

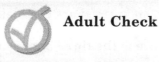 **Adult Check** _____

                                                  Initial   **Date**

 Review the material in this section in preparation for the Self Test. This Self Test will check your mastery of this particular section as well as your knowledge of the previous section.

SELF TEST 2

Complete the following activities (each answer, 3 points).

2.01   List the primary colors.

        a. _____

        b. _____

        c. _____

2.02   List the secondary colors.

        a. _____

        b. _____

        c. _____

2.03   List three elements of design.

        a. _____

        b. _____

        c. _____

2.04   List three principles of design.

        a. _____

        b. _____

        c. _____

Answer *true* **or** *false* (each answer, 3 points).

2.05   _____   Value is the lightness or darkness of a color.

2.06   _____   Purple is a warm color.

2.07   _____   The floor should be the darkest color in a room.

2.08   _____   Warm colors create a cheerful and inviting mood in a room.

2.09   _____   Value and intensity of a color can affect the appearance of room proportion.

2.010   _____   The first rocking chair was designed by the Shakers.

2.011   _____   Green and red are complementary colors.

2.012   _____   Space is the three-dimensional setting for furniture or furnishings.

2.013   _____   The decorative style known as Empire refers to the French Empire of Louis XVI.

2.014 _____ Asymmetrical balance is formal balance.

2.015 _____ The Federal style of furniture was the result of the American Revolution.

2.016 _____ Curved lines represent gentleness and quiet.

2.017 _____ One's decorating plan should include one's family's interests and activities.

2.018 _____ The bedroom should be located close to the center of activity.

2.019 _____ Doors should swing out of a room.

2.020 _____ A floor plan is the best tool for arranging furniture.

2.021 _____ One way to achieve rhythm in a room is to repeat a color, line, shape, or design.

2.022 _____ The bed is the focal point of a bedroom.

2.023 _____ Every bedroom should have at least a bed, chest of drawers, and a night stand.

Short Answer (answer, 7 points).

2.024 How did the Industrial Revolution influence interior decorating and the furniture produced in this period?

_____

_____

_____

_____

_____

80 / 100

Score _____

Adult Check _____
                Initial   Date

33

III. SPECIFIC TREATMENTS

We have seen that the proper arrangement of furniture in a room can make all the difference in the appearance, comfort, and pleasure that room offers. It is also true that rearranging the furniture is a fairly easy and an inexpensive way to change the "spirit" of the room. We have also seen that there are many styles of furniture. The materials and methods used in making furniture determine the quality and appearance of that furniture. In this section we will learn about the different kinds of wood used in making furniture.

What about the various architectural changes that need to be made? Can you change the flooring in a house? How about a wall? How about the window that has an unsightly view or a room that never gets any sun? Can these problems be solved inexpensively?

This section will also look at some ways to use some specific treatments of interior design, from floor to ceiling and from wall to wall.

Section Objectives

Review these objectives. When you have completed this section, you should be able to:

7. Gain knowledge concerning the woods used in making furniture.

8. Gain understanding in specific treatments such as floors and floor coverings, walls, windows, and lighting.

FURNITURE

In decorating, styles and colors do NOT need to match as long as they coordinate and produce an attractive appearance. The upholstery on your furniture should coordinate, with colors, patterns, and solids selected so they add to the decorative scheme of the room.

Many different types of wood are used for furniture construction. Pieces of furniture made of wood do not have to match exactly; certain finishes and stains can change the appearance of many woods. However, the wood should be similar, (dark or light), if not exactly the same. Today, it is fashionable to mix and match wood chairs at a dining room table, for example. The chairs may have similar styles, but not be exactly the same. The woods used may be different as well. The effect is especially charming when antiques are used.

Hardwoods come from trees that shed their leaves in winter: maple, oak, cherry, walnut, and mahogany. They are finer in grain, can be carved more intricately, and are usually more expensive. Softwoods, on the other hand, come from trees that retain their needles throughout the year: pine, cedar, and redwood. They are easier to work with and used to produce many good pieces of furniture. Furniture made from soft wood is usually less expensive.

Since there is such a wide variety of finishes used on wood today, it is difficult to distinguish between the different varieties. Most people select wood for its beauty, individuality, and aesthetics of grain and color. The chart that follows gives a brief dictionary of some of the woods used in making furniture.

FAMILY AND CONSUMER SCIENCE

six

LIFEPAC TEST

80 / 100

Name _____

Date _____

Score _____

FAMILY AND CONSUMER SCIENCE 06: LIFEPAC TEST

Match the terms (each answer, 2 points).

1.	_____	Napoleon	a.	Art Nouveau
2.	_____	New England	b.	Baroque
3.	_____	Spain	c.	Empire
4.	_____	Hepplewhite	d.	International style
5.	_____	Mies van der Rohe	e.	Rocking chair
6.	_____	Louis XIV	f.	Shield-back
7.	_____	Louis Tiffany	g.	Wainscot

Answer *true* **or** *false* (each answer, 2 points).

8. _____ Rococo was a famous German furniture designer.

9. _____ The first rocking chair was designed by the Shakers.

10. _____ Chippendale is known for having beautiful curves and Chinese motifs.

11. _____ Queen Anne borrowed the claw and ball design from the French.

12. _____ The colors green, blue, and purple give a room a warm, cozy feeling.

13. _____ Hardwood comes from trees that shed their leaves in the winter.

14. _____ Priscillas are a type of drape.

15. _____ Wool is the material most often used in making carpets.

16. _____ Paint appears darker on the wall than in the can.

17. _____ The main function of windows is to admit light and air.

18. _____ You would use indirect lighting for reading a book.

19. _____ The sun does not really have a significant influence on your choice of wallpaper.

20. _____ Walls in a room can be a focal point or neutral background.

21. _____ Artwork should be hung so that the bottom of the piece is just above eye level.

22. _____ The tallest object should be placed first for an asymmetrical table arrangement.

23. _____ The first thing to consider when deciding on a tabletop arrangement is the angle from which it will be viewed.

Match the terms (each answer, 2 points). Not all answers will be used.

24. _____ pieces of furniture drawn to scale   a. floor plan

25. _____ paths of movement through a room   b. analogous

26. _____ the best tool for arranging furniture   c. templates

27. _____ one-half of the color wheel   d. extended analogous

28. _____ three colors equally spaced   e. traffic patterns

                                                                            f. triad

Put the correct letter in the blank (each answer, 2 points).

29. _____ are secondary colors.
     a. Red, blue, yellow   b. Orange, green, purple
     c. Red, yellow, purple

30. Diagonal lines indicate _____ .
     a. strength and dignity   b. action, movement
     c. springiness

31. _____ is a good resilient floor covering.
     a. Wood   b. Ceramic
     c. Vinyl tile

32. _____ refers to the size of the parts of a design or to a group of objects as they relate to each other.
     a. Scale   b. Balance
     c. Color

33. The federal style of furniture was the result of the _____ .
     a. American Revolution   b. Spanish Armada
     c. Industrial Revolution

34. Which of the following is the least expensive window treatment? _____
     a. shades   b. blinds
     c. shutters

35. The _____ influenced the furniture style during the reign of Louis XVI.
     a. French Revolution   b. Excavation of Pompeii
     c. Spanish Armada

36. _____ are examples of hardwood.
     a. Maple, oak, redwood   b. Pine, cedar, redwood
     c. Mahogany, cherry, maple

37. _____ is **not** an example of a two-dimensional object.
     a. Tapestry   b. Lamp
     c. Artwork

38. _____ is most often used for making rugs.
   a. Wool   b. Olefin
   c. Acrylic

39. Which is the correct color order from lightest to darkest? _____
   a. Ceiling, wall, floor   b. Wall, ceiling, floor
   c. Floor, wall, ceiling

Match the terms (each answer, 2 points). Answers can be used more than once.

40. _____ light values   a. makes a room look larger

41. _____ large furniture pieces   b. makes a room look smaller

42. _____ windows and doors

43. _____ large patterns on wall and ceiling

44. _____ dark values

45. _____ neutral colored objects

Short Answer.

46. In sewing for home projects you need to add your own seam and hem _____ .
   (3 points)

47. Define appliqué. (3 points)

   _____

   _____

48. How did the Industrial Revolution influence interior design and the furniture produced in this period? (4 points)

   _____

   _____

   _____

   _____

Woods Used in Furniture

WOOD TYPE	DEFINITION/DESCRIPTION
APPLE	A traditional, fine-grained furniture wood. Light in color.
AVODIRE	Used much as a veneer for modern furniture. Blond with dark brown streaks.
BAMBOO	A stem of a large tropical grass used for informal furniture. Yellow in color.
BEECH	A straight-grained wood similar to maple and birch. Pale tone.
BIRCH	A hardwood often stained to resemble more expensive woods. Its natural color is light brown.
BLACK WALNUT	Fine-grained wood capable of producing a high polish. Long popular as a furniture wood to the extent that it is now overused, the tree is now rare, and the wood is expensive. Has rich grayish-brown color.
BUTTERNUT	It is similar to black walnut in grain, hardness, and ability to take a high polish. Lighter than black walnut in tone.
CEDAR	Name given to several fragrant woods. Used in chest linings in which cloth articles are stored. Also used in place of mahogany, which it resembles.
CHERRY	The reddish wood of the cherry tree. Found most often in antiques.
EBONY	Reddish-brown color. A tropical wood which can be polished to a high gloss. Used for inlays and modern furniture. Although most ebony is dark brown or black, it also comes as dark red or green.
LAUREL	A wavy-grained wood capable of being highly polished.
MAHOGANY	Most famous of furniture woods because of its beauty and use over many centuries. Imported from Latin America, Africa, and the Philippines. Has a reddish color, though some mahogany is found which is lighter in tone.
MAPLE	Hard, strong wood used for furniture veneer. Light brown.
OAK	Name of a hardwood of many dozens of species of trees. Easily carved so that its used for decorative furniture. Color depends on the species.
ROSEWOOD	Occasionally used for expensive cabinetwork. A black-streaked, reddish-brown color.
SATINWOOD	A traditional wood found mainly in antiques, especially in inlay work. Name comes from its satiny finish. Light blond color.
TEAK	A durable wood. Ranges from yellow to brown in color with fine streaks of black.
WHITE PINE	Poorly textured wood which is often painted when used for furniture. Very lightly colored.
WHITEWOOD	Name applied to several woods such as poplar, which can be easily worked. Usually used for interior shelving or the core wood of veneered furniture. When the surface is exposed, it's usually painted.
YELLOW PINE	Harder wood than white pine. Often stained to resemble oak. Yellowish color.

Answer the following.

3.1   Do pieces of furniture in a given room have to be made of the same wood? _____

3.2   How do you distinguish between hardwood and softwood trees?

      _____

      _____

3.3   Give two examples of hardwood.

      a. _____

      b. _____

3.4   Give two examples of softwood.

      a. _____

      b. _____

3.5   Which is usually more expensive, hardwood or softwood? _____

FLOOR COVERING

Floors take a tougher beating than any other surface and are, therefore, expensive to cover. In terms of appearance and durability, it is worth buying the best that you can afford. You should consider the wear and tear that a floor surface will endure as you make your choices. For example, a kitchen receives a lot of wear and it is worth buying a tile that is easy to clean, stain resistant, scuff resistant, and durable. However, most people prefer the warmth and comfort of carpet for a bedroom. Learning about the different types of floor coverings and their qualities is an important step in interior design. We will start with hard-surfaced flooring.

Hard-surface flooring includes wood, ceramic tile, brick, slate, marble, and cement. Most wood floors don't need covering. Their natural tones and grains by themselves enhance the beauty of the room. Sometimes, hardwood floors are covered by area rugs. The appearance of the wood is enhanced by the comfort of the rug.

Wood-grain is a good choice for floor coverings.

Ceramic tiles have become very popular today. These water-resistant, durable tiles come in a variety of patterns and colors and are used in many areas of the home: **foyers**, kitchens, bathrooms, family rooms, and hallways. They offer a beautiful alternative to worn carpet in heavy traffic areas such as hallways and entrances. Area rugs are once again used to add warmth and comfort.

More than 90% of the **resilient** flooring material sold today is made of vinyl. It is popular because it is very economical (less expensive than ceramic tiles), it comes in a wide selection of colors and textures, it requires minimum care (many have a "no-wax" finish), and it is very comfortable for those standing or walking on it. It too is a good covering to use on well-trod areas such as kitchens, foyers, and hallways. It comes in sheet goods as well as individual squares.

Carpeting and rugs are functional as well as decorative. They absorb noise, provide a padded surface for comfortable walking and standing, and they help keep a room cozy and warm. There is a distinction between rugs and carpets. A rug is a small or large floor covering that is often woven with a variety of decorative patterns of more than one color of fabric. A carpet is a room-size fabric floor covering.

Carpeting can be an expensive investment and may wear out in just a few years. It is important to understand the quality of carpeting before you buy it. Understanding the material used to make the carpet, the weave of the carpet, and the function of the room to be carpeted will guide you in your decisions.

Wool is one material used in carpeting. It is usually imported because American wool is too soft. Cotton is often mixed in with it to make a wool blend. Although this does lower the expense of the carpet, it also lessens its durability.

**A good Persian rug
enhances a room's decor.**

About 95% of carpets are made from synthetic fibers such as nylon, acrylic (the most popular), polyester, and olefin. They are much less expensive than wool carpets and have many excellent qualities. Synthetic carpets are colorfast, matting-resistant, moth and mildew resistant, resilient, and easy to maintain.

Carpets are woven on a heavy backing. The thicker the backing, the more durable the carpet. A thick backing also gives more cushion. Of course, the better the backing, the more expensive the carpet. The front of the carpet consist of loops that project above the backing. These loops are either "cut" or "uncut" and are called the **pile** of the carpet. The deeper the pile, the better the quality. The thicker (more loops per square inch), the better the quality. Better quality means greater durability and softer surface.

How can you economize on carpet? Decide the function of the room; the less activity, the less expensive carpeting is needed. The most expensive carpet should be reserved for that all-important room, the family room.

Answer the following.

3.6   Distinguish between a rug and carpet.

_____

_____

3.7   What material is most often used in carpeting? _____

3.8   What are two functions of carpeting?

_____

_____

3.9   Define "pile" as it relates to carpeting.

_____

_____

3.10   In what room should you use the most expensive carpet in your home? Why?

_____

_____

_____

WALL TREATMENTS

The largest background area of any room is composed of the walls and ceiling. They are a major element in the design of the room and how they are "treated" will have a tremendous influence on the room. Walls can be a focal point or a neutral background.

Wall coverings are divided into papers, fabrics, tiles, wood paneling, mirrors, and laminates. The prices within these groups vary from the cheap papers to the most expensive wood paneling or silk wall coverings.

Wall coverings are mostly used for cosmetic purposes. They are good disguisers, helping to change the apparent proportions of a room by visually enlarging or minimizing space. They can also be used to cheer up gloom, to turn the bleak into the comfortable, and to give a sense of style if none existed before. Color value is a critical factor in light absorption and reflection. Light colors are best for rooms in which you work—they are more conducive to working. In a room with a southern exposure, you might not want to use warm colors, as it will make the room appear too bright. The surface texture of the walls also needs to be considered. Smooth surfaces reflect light, while rough surfaces absorb light. You also need to consider the number and location of the windows in the room.

Mini-prints: create a sense of space in small rooms.

Large patterns on wall: plain ceiling helps retain sense of height.

Large patterns on wall and ceiling: make room seem smaller.

Geometric prints: give impression of greater space.

Vertical wood paneling: makes ceiling seem higher.

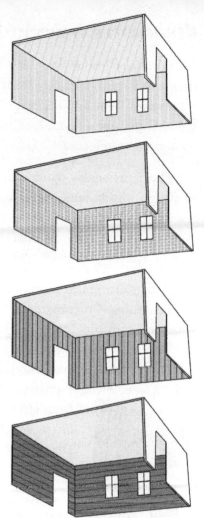

Horizontal wood paneling: makes room seem wider.

There are some general guidelines for deciding on wall treatment. Vibrant colors and large wall graphics are less formal, whereas, darker colors, subtle colors, and small, regular designs in wallpaper all present a more formal appearance.

Here are some things to consider when selecting wall coverings. Choose paint that is slightly lighter than the color you want because it will appear darker when dry. It is easiest to use pre-pasted wallpaper, but remember to prepare the wall according to the directions that come with the paper or it may not stick. Ceramic tile is used most often in the kitchen or bathroom, but can be used elsewhere if desiring a certain effect. Usually brick and stone are installed when the house is built.

Answer the following.

3.11   Walls in a room can be used as either a _____ or neutral background.

3.12   Does the sun have any significant influence over your selection of wallpaper? _____

3.13   Large patterns on the wall and ceiling make a room seem _____ .

3.14   Horizontal wood paneling makes a room seem _____ .

3.15   Should you use vibrant colors or subtle colors in the living room? _____

3.16   Paint appears _____ on the wall than in the can.

3.17   Give an example of a wall treatment other than wallpaper or paint. _____

WINDOW TREATMENTS

Windows are worthy of more serious thought than they get. They are often highly decorative by themselves and certainly form a major part of the architecture in a room. The main function of a window is to admit light and air, but windows also can be used to create an illusion of space within a room. Their size, shape, proportion, location, and relationship to other furnishings help to determine which window treatment is selected.

There are many window treatments to choose from. The selections range from drapes and curtains to shutters, blinds, shades, or even plants. Combining more than one treatment can create a delightful result. Windows of one room should be treated in the same manner to produce a more unified, coordinated effect. A house with an open floor plan does not require identical window treatments, but they should coordinate.

Drapes are more formal, elaborate, and are hung differently than curtains. Curtains usually have pockets at the top through which curtain rods are run. Drapes are pinch-pleated and hung with drapery hooks onto a rod. Drapes usually hang to the floor. A standard drapery rod is hidden behind the drapes. Drapes can also hang below and expose a decorative rod. They can be opened from either side or from the middle by a cord or pulley mechanism attached to the rod. Drapes are usually made from a heavier fabric and add a certain formality to a room.

Pinch-pleated drapery

Curtains are less formal than drapes. They may hang to the windowsill, a few inches below the sill or down to the floor. There are many different styles of curtains, a few of which are shown below.

Priscillas are the most formal curtain style. They are made of sheer fabric that either meets in the middle or creates a dramatic effect through the use of a double rod crisscross.

Café curtains hang from the rod with rings, clips, or fabric loops. This style works well in combination with wooden shutters. Shown are café curtains with two tiers.

Curtain

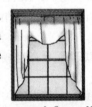

Swag with tails

Priscilla

Café curtains hung with a **swag**.

Cafe curtains

Rod pocket curtains are for doors as well as windows. They are attached to top and bottom so they do not interfere with openings and closings. They are usually of lightweight, semi-sheer fabric.

Shades come in many styles. The roll-up shade is the least expensive window treatment and can be cut to fit any window. It comes in a variety of colors and is considered less formal than other window treatments. It can be bought in "room darkening" models that block out almost all light. The most popular shades are probably the pleated shades. They are lightweight and more formal than roll-ups, costing more as well. They are also known as Duette shades or honeycomb shades.

Rod pocket curtains

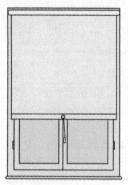

Roll-up shade

Blinds are decorative and functional. They help control light and ventilation and can be closed at varying angles to direct the light to protect your furnishings. Originally called "venetian" blinds, they are made of numerous horizontal or vertical slats of aluminum, wood, or plastic. Vertical blinds are especially popular for sliding door openings. They come in the traditional 2″ widths as well as the new 1″ mini-blind widths.

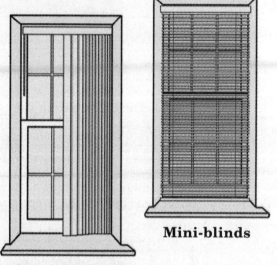

Pleated shade

Vertical blinds

Mini-blinds

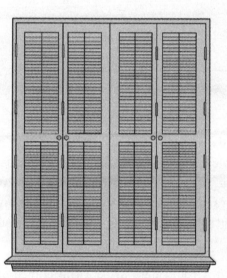

Wooden shutters

Wooden shutters can control light, provide privacy, or hide an unpleasant view.

Shutters can be painted to blend with the rest of the decor or stained in a wood tone to produce a warm effect.

Plants can be a fun way to create a unique window treatment for windows that do not require privacy. They are a pleasant alternative to the traditional window treatments.

Window with plant shelves

Window treatments have many functions. They can be decorative, provide privacy, control noise and light, and help to conserve energy.

Window treatments can either harmonize or contrast with the overall scheme of the room. They harmonize when their color is similar to that of the walls, which is important in a small room where there is already a great deal of contrast.

Contrast can be seen in color, style, or pattern. Window treatments might be hung with curves to contrast with the straight lines of the furniture. A decorative pattern can offer contrast in a room that has little pattern in the upholstery, carpeting, etc.

Window treatments can help to bring together all of the decorations of your room. Through their color, pattern, lines, and the manner in which they are hung, they can add harmony or contrast to any room.

Answer the following questions.

3.18   What is the main function of windows? _____ .

3.19   Which are more formal, drapes or curtains? _____

3.20   How do drapes and curtains differ in the way they are hung?

_____

_____

3.21   Which kind of *curtain* is the most formal? _____

3.22   What is the difference in the construction of a shade and a blind?

_____

_____

3.23   What are some of the functions of window treatment?

_____

_____

LIGHTING

Lighting is a very important element of any decor. Light can visually increase the apparent space in a room. If handled correctly, it can bring out the best features of a room and help diminish the worst ones. The amount of lighting a room has can determine the mood of the room. A well-lighted room will appear cheerful and inviting. The lighting can help to set off the interior decorations better so that you can enjoy them. The quality and effect of color is largely influenced by use of lighting. Texture, too, can be enhanced by lighting.

Make good use of natural light when possible. The amount of sun a room gets affects the choice of colors used in the decor. If a room faces south, it usually gets quite a bit of sunlight, so you should use cool colors. If the room faces north, use warm colors to brighten the room.

The amount and size of windows in a room are important considerations. If a room has a lot of windows or one large window, it will get a lot of natural light. In a room with a lot of natural light, you can pretty much decorate as you wish. But a room with little or no natural light requires brighter colors so the room will not appear gloomy.

Artificial lighting has made more dramatic progress in this country than any other element in interior design. It can be made to alter shape and color, to distort or enhance, dramatize or minimize, to increase working efficiency, and to form its own subtly changing decoration. It is easier to understand light and the various ways to manipulate it if you understand the three main types: general or background lighting, local or task lighting, and decorative lighting. Most rooms should have a combination of at least two of these types of lighting.

General or background lighting is achieved by a low level of lighting throughout the living area. This type of lighting includes ceiling fixtures, table lamps, and indirect lighting that casts light on walls and ceiling which then reflect the light into the room.

42

Local or task lighting should provide adequate illumination for all normal household activities, as well as create interesting pools of light. In living areas, the light source is usually from table, floor, or desk lamps. In kitchens, laundry, and utility rooms, it is from fixtures like **fluorescent** or **incandescent** tubes or spots over working surfaces. In bathrooms, bulbs could be installed all around a mirror as well as down lights over bathtubs and basins.

Accent or decorative lighting is the type of light used to draw attention to possessions or areas that you want to emphasize and also provides dramatic and interesting highlights.

A number of the lamp styles available are listed in the chart below.

	LAMP STYLE	*USE OR DESCRIPTION*
	High-intensity lamps and study lights	Designed to throw direct light on a work surface.
	Table lamps	Come in a wide variety of styles and sizes. They provide a major source of direct light for reading and hand work.
	Swag or hanging lamps	Not as popular as they used to be. Used not only as a light source, but also as a decorative accent.
	Pole lamps	Not as popular as they used to be. Can be easily moved from one location to another. Each lighting fixture can be individually adjusted to provide light as needed.
	Floor lamps	Some are available today with a small table attached, some with oversized shades over groups of bulbs.

	Fan and light combinations	Have replaced most other ceiling light fixtures. The fan is decorative and serves to circulate air. It provides a good source of room light.
	Period lamps	Should be used if a specific style or period decor is used in a room. They are practical, decorative, and can be an outstanding feature of a room. An antique lamp, Tiffany lamp, or Victorian lamp should have a prominent place in a room.

Answer the following.

3.24   Name two functions of lighting from a decorator's view.

_____

3.25   What are the three main types of artificial lighting?

a.   _____

b.   _____

c.   _____

3.26   What kind of lighting is best for a kitchen? _____

3.27   Which of the following emits less heat, incandescent lighting or fluorescent lighting?

_____

3.28   An antique lamp is a good example of which of the three types of artificial lighting?

_____

Review the material in this section in preparation for the Self Test. This Self Test will check your mastery of this particular section as well as your knowledge of the previous sections.

SELF TEST 3

Choose the correct answer (each answer, 4 points).

3.01   _____ is **not** an example of a hardwood.

a. Maple   b. Cedar
c. Cherry

3.02   _____ is **not** an example of a softwood.
a. Pine   b. Oak
c. Redwood

3.03   Which of the following statements is **not** true about hardwood? _____
    a. comes from trees that shed their leaves in the winter
    b. comes from trees that keep their leaves all year long
    c. is usually more expensive

3.04   _____ is a good, resilient floor covering.
    a. Wood   b. Ceramic tile
    c. Vinyl tile

3.05   The _____ should have the most expensive carpet.
    a. master bedroom   b. family room
    c. dining room

3.06   _____ are primary colors.
    a. Red, blue, yellow   b. Orange, green, purple
    c. Red, yellow, purple

3.07   The brightness or darkness of a color is the _____ of that color.
    a. value   b. intensity
    c. tint

3.08   Diagonal lines indicate _____ .
    a. strength and dignity   b. action, movement
    c. boldness

3.09   _____ shows a pleasing relationship among all parts to each other and to the design as a whole.
    a. Scale   b. Balance
    c. Proportion

3.010   A _____ is the first and best tool for arranging furniture.
    a. template   b. floor plan
    c. architectural degree

3.011   The Federal style of furniture was the result of the _____ .
    a. Industrial Revolution   b. American Revolution
    c. Spanish Armada

3.012   _____ is **not** an example of a curtain.
    a. Café   b. Pinch-pleat
    c. Priscilla

3.013   _____ are the least expensive window treatment.
    a. Shades   b. Blinds
    c. Shutters

3.014   The "rococo" style of furniture was developed during the reign of _____ .
    a. Louis XIV   b. Louis XV
    c. Louis XVI

3.015 _____ is known for the shield back chair design.
      a. Hitchcock   b. Hepplewhite
      c. Duncan Phyfe

Complete the following (each answer, 5 points).

3.016   What are two functions of a carpet?

      a. _____

      b. _____

3.017   What are two functions of window treatments?

      a. _____

      b. _____

3.018   What are two functions of lighting?

      a. _____

      b. _____

Answer *true* **or** *false* (each answer 1 point).

3.019   _____ Furniture with different kinds of wood can be used in the same room.

3.020   _____ Wool is the material most often used in making carpets.

3.021   _____ Mini-prints create a sense of space in a room.

3.022   _____ Paint appears darker dried on the wall than in the can.

3.023   _____ Plants may be used as a window covering.

3.024   _____ The main function of windows is to let light and air in.

3.025   _____ Local lighting is the preferred lighting for the kitchen.

3.026   _____ You would use indirect lighting for reading a book.

3.027   _____ Walls in a room can be a focal point or neutral background.

3.028   _____ The sun does not really have a significant influence on your choice of wallpaper.

80 / 100

Score   _____

Adult Check   _____
                            Initial   Date

IV. VISUAL ENRICHMENT

Once the framework of a room is completed, the decorating done to satisfaction, and the furniture chosen, it is time to concentrate on putting together the sort of arrangements and decorative objects that will make a room seem both distinctive and memorable. These visual enrichments fall into two categories: two-dimensional and three-dimensional objects.

Section Objectives

Review these objectives. When you have completed this section, you should be able to:

9. Demonstrate skill in producing visual enrichment through two-dimensional and three-dimensional objects.

10. Document in a notebook how you would design your bedroom.

TWO-DIMENSIONAL OBJECTS

Two-dimensional objects include pictures, photographs, mirrors, and a wide variety of wall hangings. Your selections should enhance the appearance of the room, not just fill up space. Accessories that can be functional as well as decorative provide atmosphere and reflect the tastes and interests of the people who live there. They can and should be changed from time to time, based on your interests.

Select artwork that you like. Avoid choosing artwork that blends in with or matches the color of the upholstery and drapes. If it does, it becomes merely a decorative addition rather than an object of interest.

Before selecting artwork for your home, you should become familiar with the variety of mediums from which you can choose. Most people think high, unreachable expensive masterpieces when "original art" is mentioned. But it is possible to find original art for reasonable prices. Watercolor paintings tend to be less expensive than oil paintings.

Reproductions should be avoided because they are usually dull and lackluster in comparison to originals. However original graphic prints, such as **etchings** or **silk-screens**, are works of art that artists create and print in a limited number of copies. Other forms of original artwork include charcoal, pastel, and pen-and-ink drawings. These range in price, according to their quality and the renown of the artist. Once again, the key is to shop around until you find something you like.

Embroidery, needlepoint, and certain types of tapestries are examples of artistic craftwork that can be hung like paintings. Many of these items you could make yourself with do-it-yourself kits found at craft stores.

Photographs may also have a place in your home. Because they are usually small, they should be hung in a smaller space or over a less important piece of furniture. They can be attractively displayed in groupings as well.

Mirrors are functional as well as decorative. In a hallway, bedroom, or bathroom they are hung primarily for practical reasons. They are used in other rooms as a decorative piece because of their shape or frame. What they reflect also adds to their interest. A glance at a mirror that reflects a beautiful picture or an attractively decorated wall is interesting.

Arranging two-dimensional objects requires planning and practice. Focus on the principles of design: balance, rhythm, color, and proportion. Balance is important in the arrangement of the artwork. Symmetrical balance is most often used in wall arrangements. The way the artwork is hung should draw the eyes down and into the room (rhythm). Proportion is in both the relationships of the sizes of the artwork to each other in an arrangement and the sizes of the artwork to the furniture in the room. Artwork is an excellent way to tie together the various colors among the wall and other objects in the room. You will eventually develop an eye for arrangement that has a pleasing effect on the overall design of the room.

Large works of art can be hung singly or (if the same size) in pairs. Smaller works can be hung in massed groups.

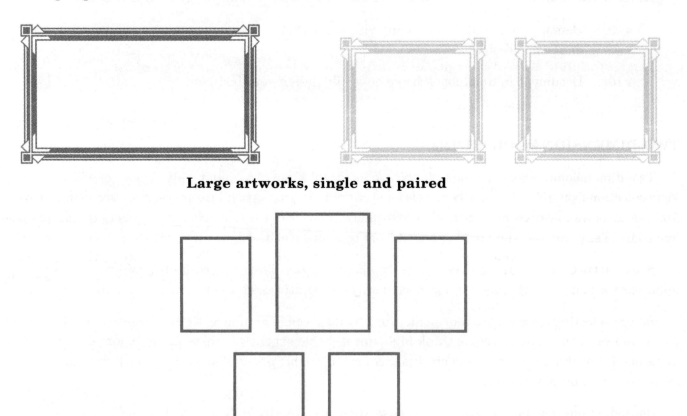

Large artworks, single and paired

Smaller artworks, massed group

Several different sizes of artworks can also be grouped in an attractive balanced manner.

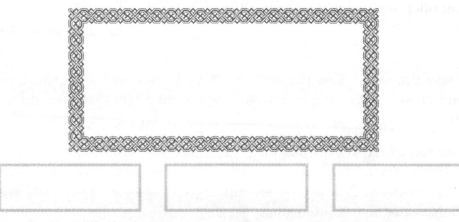

Smaller artworks with one large artwork

Small works of art can be combined in an agreeable arrangement with one large painting.

Pictures are meant to be looked at. Therefore, the bottom of the artwork should be slightly below eye level. This is an approximate guide. It will vary according to the height of the ceiling and the objects along a wall.

To hang a grouping of pictures, lay them on a large sheet of paper. After you are satisfied with your arrangement, outline each separate picture. Now tape the paper to the wall where you want the arrangement to be and hammer a straight pin or needle at the top-center of each picture. Carefully remove the paper and replace the marking pin or needle with a picture hanger. Check the back of each picture to see how much allowance is needed for the wire or hook, for it may adjust where you need to put the picture hanger in order to keep the arrangement as you designed it.

Answer the following.

4.1   Is it appropriate to change decorative accessories from time to time? _____

4.2   Is it possible to obtain reasonably priced original artwork? _____

4.3   Why is it best to avoid purchasing reproductions?

_____

_____

4.4   What are original graphic prints?

_____

4.5   Give an example of craftwork that can be hung on the wall. _____

4.6   How can mirrors add to the decor of the room?

_____

4.7   What is the best way to determine how high a piece of artwork should be placed on the wall?

_____

_____

4.8   What is wrong with the artwork grouping below?

_____

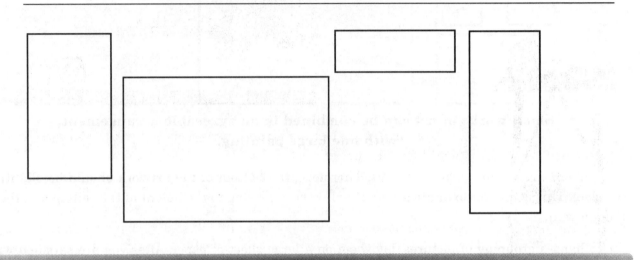

THREE-DIMENSIONAL OBJECTS

There are many other kinds of objects to display in your home. Vases, candlesticks, figurines, clocks, carvings, lamps, pillows, plants, and floral arrangements are three-dimensional objects with interesting shapes, decorative designs, and exquisite colors. Learning to add these to your decor will enhance the effect and express your individuality, bringing your personality into the room.

Once you have selected the items you want to display, you are ready to arrange your display. Tabletop arrangements are three-dimensional, just like furniture. You first need to determine from which angle the arrangement will be viewed. If it is a coffee table, you will be looking down on your arrangement; if it is a fireplace mantel, the view will be closer to eye level. If the arrangement is on a dining room table, then it will be viewed from all around. The more angles and sides from which an arrangement will be viewed, the simpler the arrangement should be.

The simplest arrangement is symmetrical, meaning that one side of the arrangement is equal to the other. A clock in the center of a mantel with matching candlesticks on each side is a good example of a symmetrical arrangement.

In asymmetrical arrangements, the right and left sides are not identical but they should remain in balance. Place the taller object first and then arrange the smaller pieces around it, moving them around until you feel the arrangement is balanced.

If a lamp is part of the arrangement (it is if it is on the table), it should be placed first. It should be placed so the best illumination is guaranteed. All other objects will be arranged around the lamp.

Selecting and arranging the various accessories that will add visual enrichment to your room is not a difficult task if you are willing to put a little time and thought into it. Be creative and have fun.

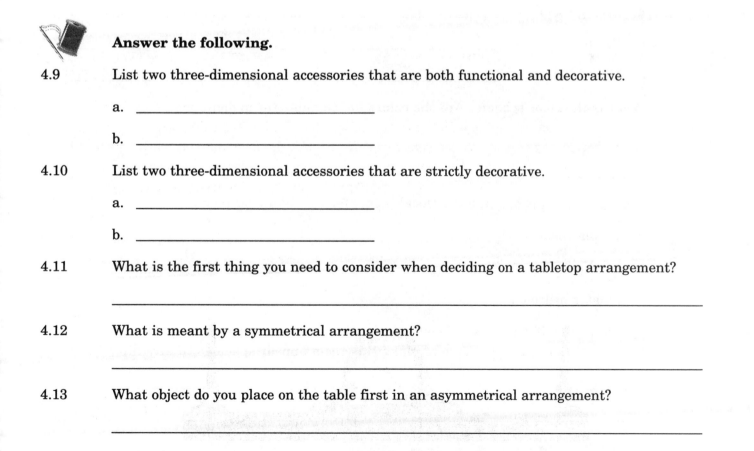

Answer the following.

4.9   List two three-dimensional accessories that are both functional and decorative.

    a. _____

    b. _____

4.10   List two three-dimensional accessories that are strictly decorative.

    a. _____

    b. _____

4.11   What is the first thing you need to consider when deciding on a tabletop arrangement?

    _____

4.12   What is meant by a symmetrical arrangement?

    _____

4.13   What object do you place on the table first in an asymmetrical arrangement?

    _____

Complete the following activity.

4.14 Now that you have completed the information sections of this LIFEPAC you are ready to put your knowledge to the test. Arrange to visit a group of model homes in your area. Complete the follow questionnaire.

Home Economics Interior Decorating Field Trip Questionnaire

Name _____ Date _____ Model _____

Choose one model and answer the following questions.

1. List any *period* pieces of furniture.

   _____

   _____

2. Is wainscot used anywhere in the house? If so, where?

   _____

3. What is the style of furniture?

   a. Living room   _____

   b. Kitchen   _____

   c. Master bedroom _____

4. What is the color scheme? Are the colors harmonious throughout the house?

   _____

   _____

5. What is the point of emphasis (focal point) for the following rooms:

   a. Living room   _____

   b. Kitchen   _____

   c. Master bedroom _____

6. Check to see if there is a good relationship between form and space in the master bedroom. What has been done to make this room appear spacious (if anything)?

   _____

   _____

7. Is the master bedroom large enough to accommodate appropriate furniture (at least a queen size bed, dresser, night stands, etc.)? Is there enough storage space? What kind of closets (walk-in, linen, his/her)? If not, explain.

_____

_____

8. Is there adequate storage and closet space throughout the house? If not, explain.

_____

_____

9. The traffic pattern is the walkway from the door of the room to the major pieces of furniture, the closets, and the windows. Is it sufficient throughout the house? If not, explain.

_____

_____

10. Is there adequate lighting in the house? If not, explain.

_____

_____

11. Is there a family room as well as a living room or is there a great room? A great room is a large room that combines the family room and the living room.

_____

_____

12. Is there a foyer (entrance)? _____

13. How many bathrooms are there? _____

14. Is there a formal dining area? _____ Is there an informal dining area or breakfast nook? _____

15. Are there adequate electrical outlets and phone plugs throughout the house? _____

16. List the types of floor coverings.

	Color	Type
a. Living room	_____	_____
b. Kitchen	_____	_____
c. Foyer	_____	_____
d. Master Bedroom and Bath	_____	_____

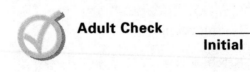

Adult Check _____

                         Initial   **Date**

Note: If a student does not have model homes available, she could critique her own home or the home of a friend. There are also new home websites available that have pictures of model homes.

17.   What kind of wall treatment?

	Color	Type
a. Living room	_____	_____
b. Kitchen	_____	_____
c. Foyer	_____	_____
d. Master Bedroom	_____	_____

18.   What kind of window treatment?

	Color	Type
a. Living room	_____	_____
b. Kitchen	_____	_____
c. Foyer	_____	_____
d. Master Bedroom	_____	_____

19.   What has been used for visual enrichment (accessories that are both functional as well as decorative)?

_____

_____

20.   How many people could comfortably live in this house? _____

 Adult Check _____

                                                 Initial   **Date**

Note: If a student does not have model homes available, she could critique her own home or the home of a friend. There are also new home websites available that have pictures of model homes.

Finish your Design Notebook.

4.15   Hopefully your field trip was a fascinating and informative experience. Your interior design notebook should already contain the following:

    a.   Drawings of your bedroom floor plan—Activity 2.38 and Activity 2.39
    b.   Pictures of your furniture choices—Activity 2.40
    c.   Templates of furniture choices—Activity 2.41
    d.   Critique of present bedroom—Activity 2.42
    e.   Several floor plan and template arrangements—Activity 2.43

Now you are ready to complete your interior design notebook by completing the following activities. For these activities, you can use pictures taken from magazines, catalogs, sales pamphlets, or personal photographs to exemplify the affect you are creating. If at all possible, it is best if you can include actual samples of each specific treatment. Many stores such as home improvement, wallpaper, paint, carpet, and tile stores have free samples of their products. Use descriptions only to expand on the samples and pictures. Choosing a theme such as sports, dolls, flowers, marine life, country, American, or a special color scheme can really be fun. So, get creative and begin.

Choose a theme that reflects your personality.

For all steps, glue or secure your pictures and samples onto paper or place them in a zippered plastic bag in your notebook.

    f.   Floor covering(s). Include the color and type for your selection of tile (i.e. ceramic or vinyl), wood (i.e., oak or man-made) or carpet (i.e. Berber or pile). Include any area rugs you might be using.

    g.   Wall covering(s). Include swatches of wallpaper or paint color if possible. Also include pictures of or a sample of paneling where available.

    h.   Window treatments. If you have a special type of window, you should also include a picture of the window (i.e., bay window, double panel window with enclosed mini-blinds, window seat, etc.)

    i.   Lighting: lamps, natural, ceiling fixtures, or ceiling-fan/light combination, etc.

    j.   Samples, pictures, or description of bed treatments. Bedspread, shams, pillows, stuffed animals, canopy, comforter, and bed ruffle are examples of what you will choose from for your bed.

k. Pictures or descriptions of the visual enrichments you have selected. Remember, if you have established a theme or a color scheme, you need to follow through with your accessories. Contrast and color spot matches are very effective.

Parent or Instructor: This assignment is only a planning assignment. The student is not required to purchase anything or change his room. Call it a "dream book" if you will. It is a teaching tool, so that someday when they are ready to actually decorate a home they will know the steps and techniques for accomplishing the task with skill and confidence.

Adult Check _____

Initial   Date

 Review the material in this section in preparation for the Self Test. This Self Test will check your mastery of this particular section as well as your knowledge of the previous sections.

SELF TEST 4

Write the correct letter on the blank (each answer 5 points).

4.01 _____ influenced the furniture style during the reign of Louis XVI.
    a. The French Revolution   b. The excavation of Pompeii
    c. The Spanish Armada

4.02 What feature did the Queen Anne-style of furniture borrow from the French? _____
    a. cabriole leg   b. shield-back chair
    c. tubular construction

4.03 _____ is **not** a result of the Industrial Revolution.
    a. Federal style of furniture   b. Furniture made by machine
    c. Better quality of furniture

4.04 Three colors evenly spaced on the color wheel produces a(n) _____ color scheme.
    a. analogous   b. triadic
    c. complementary

4.05 Paths of movement through a room are called _____ .
    a. traffic patterns   b. floor plans
    c. templates

4.06 _____ are principles of design.
    a. Proportion, balance, rhythm   b. Proportion, scale, space
    c. Scale, form, space

4.07 _____ are examples of hardwood.
    a. Maple, oak, redwood   b. Cedar, pine, walnut
    c. Mahogany, cherry, maple

4.08 _____ is **not** an example of a three dimensional object.
    a. Picture frame   b. Lamp
    c. Artwork

4.09 _____ is **least** often used for making rugs.
    a. Wool   b. Olefin
    c. Acrylic

4.010 Which of the following affects your choice of wallpaper? _____
    a. the sun   b. size of room
    c. personal preference   d. all of the above.

Answer *true* **or** *false* (each answer, 5 points).

4.011 _____ Change your decorative accessories from time to time.

4.012 _____ It is nearly impossible to buy original artwork for a reasonable price.

4.013 _____ Reproductions should be avoided.

4.014 _____ A tapestry is a three-dimensional object.

4.015 _____ Artwork should be hung so that the bottom of the piece is just above eye level.

4.016 _____ A clock is a three-dimensional object that can be decorative as well as functional.

4.017 _____ The tallest object should be placed first in an asymmetrical arrangement.

4.018 _____ The first thing to consider when deciding on a tabletop arrangement is the angle from which it will be viewed.

4.019 _____ When arranging several pieces of artwork on the wall the tops of the artwork must be even.

4.020 _____ Large works of art can be hung in pairs if they are the same size.

 Score _____

Adult Check _____
Initial   Date

V. SEWING FOR THE HOME

There are a variety of items that you can sew for your home: **slipcovers**, pillow covers, bedspreads, curtains, draperies, and table linens. This section will give a brief overview of what each of these entail. You will have the opportunity to make a pillow for your bedroom as well.

Section Objectives

Review these objectives. When you have completed this section, you should be able to:

11.   Learn the basics about sewing for the home.

12.   Design and sew a pillow that will complement the decor of your newly designed bedroom.

A BRIEF OVERVIEW

Although the same basic sewing skills that you learned for dressmaking are used in sewing for the home, they are often applied differently. For example, the "pattern" for cutting out slipcover fabric may be the upholstered chair or sofa being covered. With draperies and curtains, the pattern is just a set of key measurements.

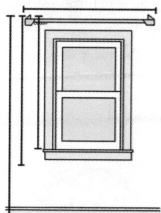

In most home projects, you need to add your own seam and hem allowances. It is usually easier to machine stitch most projects because many of them involve handling large quantities of material at one time. This is heavy and awkward if done by hand. Machine sewing is faster and usually results in a more durable product.

Fabrics called "decorator fabrics" are made especially for home sewing projects. They are normally 45 inches wide and often treated to resist wrinkles, stains, or fading. Choosing the proper fabric involves relating the weight and weave of the fabric to the wear the fabric will get, the construction methods that will be used and the final appearance you want from it. For example, a slipcover fabric should have a close enough weave so that it will be durable and hold its shape over time. Also consider the color, design and texture of the fabric, to see how it will blend with the rest of the decor. Finally, consider the cost of the fabric. Make sure that the expense and time invested are worth tackling the job yourself. In addition to your basic equipment, consider other tools that might come in handy when sewing for the home. See the chart.

Equipment and Supplies recommended for Home Sewing Projects

✔ Heavy duty sewing shears

✔ T-pins

✔ Carpenter's folding rule

✔ Heavy duty machine needle (depending on fabric)

✔ Notions—heavy-duty zippers for use in slipcovers, pillow forms, metal weight for draperies, pleater tapes, and hooks.

A few decorative sewing techniques can add interest to many of the things you sew for the home. **Appliqué** is a technique whereby small piece(s) of fabric are applied as decorative trimming by hand or machine. Choose fabric that is light to medium weight and has a smooth surface. You can really be creative with appliqué, using geometric designs, flowers, initials, and simple objects to create personal and unique decorations.

Quilting is another popular decorative sewing technique. It is used mostly to make bed coverings (quilts) and pillows. The basic quilting technique involves a simple running stitch used to anchor a soft filler between two layers of fabric. The top fabric can be anything, but the most ideal fabric is lightweight and smooth. The bottom fabric layer traditionally was **muslin**, but now can be anything. (I have found that bed sheets work well because they are wide, avoiding seams in the middle of the quilt and there are so many beautiful patterns available.) The middle layer is commonly a polyester batting, although **down** is not uncommon. There are many types of quilting from the crisscross diagonal or diamond stitching to the charming beauty of overlapping circles.

Trapunto is a type of quilting in which only the design part is padded leaving an **embossed** design. It gives a plain colored quilt interest with a more elegant and formal appearance. It is also fun to stitch around a pattern such as an animal or flower and stuff them for a more interesting look.

A slipcover is a practical and economical way to restore a worn piece of furniture or to give it a new look. If you are replacing an old cover, carefully remove it and use it as the pattern for cutting the fabric for the new one. If starting fresh, fabric requirements are figured by measuring the piece of furniture, then adding yardage for any specific requirements such as the cover's skirt or making cording for the seams.

There are three types of bedspreads: throw, flounced, and tailored. A throw is a flat piece that drapes over the bed. The flounced is fitted and has drop sides that are pleated or gathered. The tailored is a fitted and has drop sides that are straight. Accessories that can be made to enhance the beauty and interest of the bed are throw pillows, shams, and bed skirts (usually used with comforters that do not reach the floor).

Throw bedspread   **Flounced bedspread**   **Tailored bedspread**

Table linens can be made in their entirety or can be embroidered, cross-stitched, or **tatted** onto a ready-made linen. Tablecloths, napkins, placemats, center pieces, and table runners can all be given that personal touch.

Sewing for the home can be a fun and satisfying experience. It gives you the opportunity to take a meaningful, active part in decorating your home.

Answer the following.

5.1   How do the patterns for slipcovers differ from patterns used in dressmaking?

_____

_____

5.2   In most home projects you need to add your own seam and hem _____ .

5.3   When you have a sewing project for the home what kind of fabrics do you ask for at the cloth store? _____

5.4   What are decorator fabrics treated to resist?

_____

_____

5.5   Define appliqué.

_____

5.6   _____ is a type of quilting in which only the design part is padded.

5.7   What are the three types of bedspreads?

a.   _____

b.   _____

c.   _____

PILLOW PROJECT

One of the most popular and creative ways to accessorize a room with little expense and a minimum amount of work is with pillows. Whether it is for a piece of furniture, a bed, or the floor, a pillow can be both functional and decorative.

There are basically two types of pillows: knife edge pillows and box edge pillows. The knife edge pillow is thickest at the center and tapers off to the edges. It can be almost any shape. A box edge pillow has uniform thickness from the center to the edges and has a side depth that must be covered with a **boxing strip**. The **bolster** is a type of box edge pillow. The most familiar shapes of box edge pillows are rectangular, circular, circular bolster, and wedge bolster.

Making pillow covers can be done with a pre-made pillow form or by making a shaped fabric covering and stuffing it with batting.

61

If trim is going to be applied to a pillow, it should be added before sewing the two sides together. Ruffles, cording and lace are a few trims that can be added to the seams of a pillow. Appliqué, quilting, or trapunto on the front side of the pillow can enhance its beauty and help it blend in with the rest of the room's decor. Pillows in shapes of animals, balls, flowers, etc. can tie together the theme or color scheme of a room.

Making a knife edge pillow is quite simple.

✔ Design and cut the fabric into the desired shape.

> ✔ If you are stuffing your pillow with batting, plan for the size you wish.

> ✔ If you are using a pre-made pillow form, take careful measurements. Measure both the width and length of the pillow form and add seam allowances to all edges.

✔ Apply all appliqués, quilting, trapunto, ribbons, buttons, bows, or any designs that need to be stitched on the front side of the pillow now.

✔ Baste the trim to the right side of the cover top along the seam line. Allow for extra trim for turning corners if you want a nice right angle corner. If you are planning a curved corner there should be less problem.

✔ With right sides together, *baste* around the pillow cover leaving an opening large enough to either stuff with batting or insert pillow form. Be careful not to catch any decorations or trims in the seam.

✔ Turn the pillow right side out to check that all is well. Make sure that all lace, trim, appliqués, etc. are not caught incorrectly in the seam. If so, open the seam at the point of the problem only and adjust.

✔ Stitch the seam.

✔ Clip the corners and trim the seams.

✔ Turn right side out, stuff, and slip stitch the opening shut.

Complete the following activity.

5.8   Design and make a knife-edge pillow that will complement the decor of your newly designed bedroom. *Follow through with your theme or color scheme as you choose.

*If you are unable to actually redecorate your room, design your pillow to complement your present bedroom. Also, you may sew a box-edge pillow if you have the sewing skills and prefer that style.

 **Adult Check**   _____

                                 Initial   **Date**

    Although there is no Self Test for this section, the student will be held responsible for any information given in the LIFEPAC test.

Before taking the LIFEPAC Test, you may want to do one or more of these self checks.

1. _____   Read the objectives. Check to see if you can do them.
2. _____   Restudy the material related to any objectives that you cannot do.
3. _____   Use the SQ3R study procedure to review the material.
4. _____   Review activities, Self Tests and LIFEPAC vocabulary words.
5. _____   Restudy areas of weakness indicated by the last Self Test.

GLOSSARY

appliqué. Small pieces of fabric applied as decorative trimming by hand or machine.

baroque. Seventeenth-century design of European origin that stressed ornate and exaggerated forms. Important component of William and Mary and Queen Anne styles.

bolster. A long cushion or pillow for a bed, sofa, etc.

boxing strip. A strip of material that forms the sides of a box pillow.

brocade. A fabric woven with a raised overall pattern; formal.

chaise lounge. A couch or day bed in the form of a reclining chair with the seat lengthened to make a complete leg rest.

chintz. A printed cotton fabric; a painted or stained calico from India; informal.

cerulean. Sky blue.

cornucopia. A horn-shaped container filled with flowers and fruit.

down. The soft first plumage of many young birds.

eclecticism. The use of what seems best from various sources.

embellishment. An ornament or decoration.

emboss. To raise (surface design); to cause to bulge out.

emphasis. Stress placed on what is important.

etching. Artwork; made by coating a metal plate with an acid resistant substance, scratching an image through with a sharp tool, and then exposing the metal to acid. The acid eats away the unprotected areas of the plate.

fluorescent. Radiating light source that produces much less heat then incandescent lighting; cost less to operate; is safer for enclosed areas such as a hutch or bookcase.

fluting. Parallel horizontal concave channels used as a decorative finish.

focal point. The central or principle point of interest or attention.

foyer. Entrance hall in a home.

incandescent. Light bulb that emits light due to glowing material; gives off a yellow light which lends a golden tone to objects and produces a warm, comfortable effect.

inlay. A decorative treatment set into the surface that uses wood or other material to form texture in bands of color (stringing); pictorial images (marquetry); or geometric shapes (parquetry).

gild. To coat with gold, gold leaf, or a gold-colored substance.

gilt. The gold or other material applied in gilding.

marquetry. Inlaid work of various colored woods or other materials.

motif. A recurring subject, theme, idea, etc.; or a recurring form, shape, or figure, etc., in a design.

muslin. A cotton fabric made in various degrees of fineness and often printed, woven, or embroidered in patterns.

neoclassic. Nineteenth century trend in furniture design that sought inspiration from antiquity. Progressed through three stages in America: Federal, Empire, and Restoration.

panetiere. French Provincial style of furniture; a cabinet for storing bread.

pile. The cut or uncut loops that project above the back of a carpet.

proportion. A pleasing relationship among parts, resulting in harmony to the design as a whole.

resilient. Returning to its original form after being bent, compressed, or stretched.

rococo. Style originating in France, marked by free-form ornamental curvilinear shapes. It was a component of the Chippendale style in England and America.

scale. The size of the parts of a design or a group of objects in comparison to each other.

silkscreen. A print made by forcing ink through a stencil which is held in place by silk fabric.

slip cover. An easily removed cloth cover for a piece of furniture.

space. A three-dimensional setting for furniture and furnishings.

sphinx. A figure of an imaginary creature having a human or animal head on the body of a lion.

splat. A broad, flat piece of wood, either pierced or solid, forming the center upright part of a chair back.

stucco. An exterior finish for masonry or frame walls, usually composed of cement, sand, and hydrated lime mixed with water and laid on wet.

swag. One or more pieces of fabric draped over a rod typically used at the top of a window treatment. Often used with a pleated or tapered tail down either side.

tapestry. A fabric consisting of a warp upon which colored threads are woven by hand to produce a design, often pictorial, used for wall hangings, furniture covering, etc.

tatting. The process of making a kind of knotted lace of cotton or linen thread with a shuttle.

texture. The surface covering of fabrics, furniture, and furnishings.

veneer. A very thin layer of wood or other material for facing or inlaying wood.

BIBLIOGRAPHY

Fitzgerald, Oscar P., *Four Centuries of American Furniture*, Wallace-Homestead Book Company, Pennsylvania, 1995.

Lucie-Smith, Edward, *Furniture, a Concise History*, Oxford University Press, NY, 1979.

Petraglia, Patricia P., *Sotheby's Guide to American Furniture*, A Fireside Book, published by Simon and Schuster, NY, 1995.

Reader's Digest Complete Guide to Sewing, 11th printing, The Reader's Digest association, Inc., New York, 1985.

Reid, William and Reksten, Diane, *Interiors, An Introduction to Design and Decoration*, J. Weston Walch, Publisher, 1987.

The Encyclopedia American International, Ed. Vol. 12, Grolier Inc., Connecticut, 1997.

BEDROOM TEMPLATES

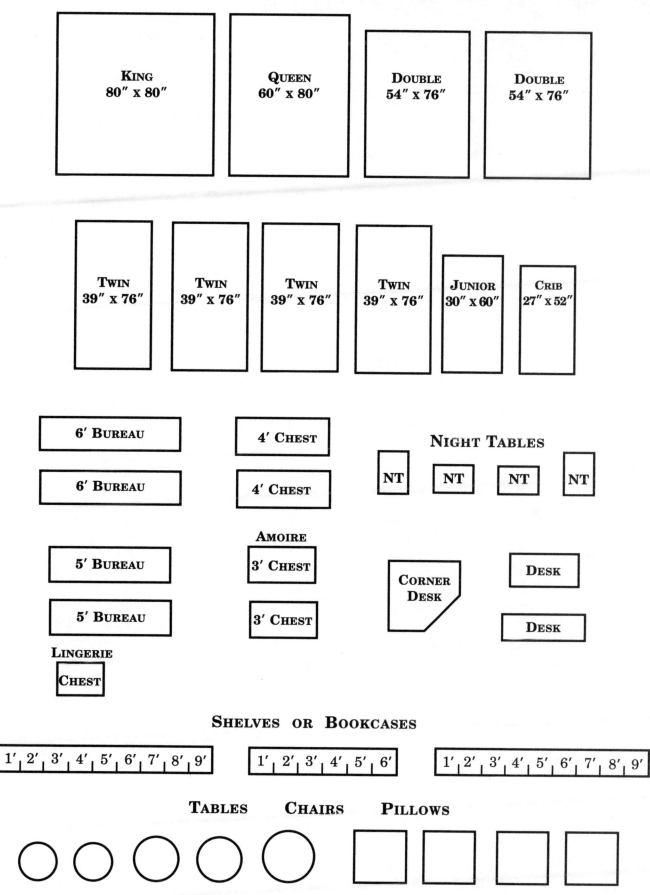

KING
80" x 80"

QUEEN
60" x 80"

DOUBLE
54" x 76"

DOUBLE
54" x 76"

TWIN
39" x 76"

TWIN
39" x 76"

TWIN
39" x 76"

TWIN
39" x 76"

JUNIOR
30" x 60"

CRIB
27" x 52"

6' BUREAU

6' BUREAU

4' CHEST

4' CHEST

NIGHT TABLES

NT   NT   NT   NT

5' BUREAU

5' BUREAU

AMOIRE

3' CHEST

3' CHEST

CORNER
DESK

DESK

DESK

LINGERIE

CHEST

SHELVES OR BOOKCASES

1' 2' 3' 4' 5' 6' 7' 8' 9'

1' 2' 3' 4' 5' 6'

1' 2' 3' 4' 5' 6' 7' 8' 9'

TABLES   CHAIRS   PILLOWS

67

FLOOR PLAN SYMBOLS

INSIDE WALL—any length x 4′ wide found between 2 rooms or between a room and a hallway

OUTSIDE WALL—any length x 6′ wide wider than an inside wall, doors and windows found on these walls

REGULAR WINDOW—found on an outside wall —sizes can vary

BAY WINDOW

BOW WINDOW

PASSAGE WAY—any length x 4′ wide found between 2 rooms or between a room and a hallway

Door/Doorway—2 ½′ or 3′

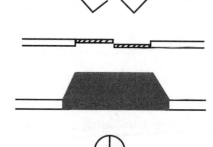

Louvre doors

Sliding doors

Fireplace

Lamp

Overhead lamp

Once you have drawn an accurate floor plan you may use it for several different arrangements, with the help of tracing paper.